Sandy Leitch
6 Margaret Street
Avoch.

23/7/45

The Victory Book

DEDICATED TO ALL THE
PEOPLES OF THE WORLD
WHO KEPT THE FLAME OF
FREEDOM BURNING IN
MANKIND'S DARKEST HOUR

ODHAMS PRESS LTD. - LONG ACRE - LONDON, W.C.2

HIS MAJESTY KING GEORGE VI
in the uniform of an Admiral of the Fleet
After the painting by
Oswald Birley, R.O.I.

UNCONDITIONAL SURRENDER

ON Tuesday, May 8, 1945, Mr. Winston Churchill broadcast to the millions of listeners in Great Britain and the British Empire the following Victory message :—

"Yesterday morning at 2.41 a.m. at Headquarters, General Jodl, the representative of the German High Command, and of Grand Admiral Dönitz, the designated head of the German State, signed the pact of unconditional surrender of all German land, sea and air forces in Europe to the Allied Expeditionary Force, and simultaneously to the Russian High Command.

Tedder Goes to Berlin

"General Bedell Smith, Chief of Staff of the Allied Expeditionary Force, and General François Sevez signed the document on behalf of the Supreme Commander of the Allied Expeditionary Force, and General Susloparov signed on behalf of the Russian High Command. Today this agreement will be ratified in Berlin, where Air Chief Marshal Tedder, Deputy Supreme Commander of the Allied Expeditionary Force, and General de Lattre de Tassigny will sign on behalf of General Eisenhower. Marshal Zhukov will sign on behalf of the Soviet High Command. The German representative will be Field-Marshal Keitel, Chief of the High Command, and the Commanders-in-Chief of the German Army, Navy and Air Forces.

" Hostilities will end officially at one minute after midnight tonight (Tuesday), but in the interests of saving lives the 'Cease Fire' began yesterday to be sounded all along the front, and our dear Channel Islands are also to be freed today . . . Today, perhaps, we shall think mostly of ourselves. To-morrow we shall pay a particular tribute to our Russian comrades whose prowess in the field has been one of the grand contributions to the general victory. The German war is therefore at an end.

"After years of preparation, Germany hurled herself upon Poland . . . and in pursuance of our guarantee to Poland, and in agreement with the French Republic, Great Britain, the British Empire and Commonwealth of Nations, declared war upon this foul aggression. After gallant France had been struck down, we, from this island and our united Empire, maintained the struggle single-handed for a whole year until we were joined by the military might of Soviet Russia and later by the overwhelming power and resources of the United States of America.

Britain's Gratitude

"Finally, almost the whole world was combined against the evil-doers who are now prostrate before us. Our gratitude to our splendid allies goes forth from all our hearts in this island and throughout the British Empire.

"We may allow ourselves a brief period of rejoicing, but let us not forget for a moment the toil and efforts that lie ahead. Japan, with all her treachery and greed, remains unsubdued. The injury she has inflicted on Great Britain, the United States, and other countries, and her detestable cruelties, call for justice and retribution. We must now devote all our strength and resources to the completion of our task, both at home and abroad. Advance, Britannia ! Long live the cause of Freedom! God Save the King!"

VICTORY CELEBRATIONS
Peace in Europe
Crowds in Trafalgar Square listen
to Mr. Churchill's Broadcast on
VE Day

FREE WORLD REJOICES

Ews of Germany's unconditional surrender was made known on the evening of Monday, May 7, and the country had already given itself over to rejoicing when, on the following afternoon, the Prime Minister briefly broadcast the official announcement of the cessation of hostilities. Mr. Churchill then went to the House of Commons to repeat the news, and was given a great ovation by a packed house which, on his suggestion, then adjourned to St. Margaret's Church, Westminster, for a service of thanksgiving.

Throughout Tuesday crowds had been pouring into the capital—happy crowds of singing, dancing people. They packed the streets, and when Mr. Churchill appeared on a balcony in Whitehall with his Cabinet colleagues and service chiefs, they cheered again and again. Later, the crowds surged down to Buckingham Palace to see the King and Queen and the two Princesses

who appeared many times on the balcony to acknowledge them.

Wednesday, May 9, was also a holiday, and again London was the scene of great rejoicing. Thousands lined the streets to see the Royal Family touring the badly bombed districts of London, and to see Mr. Churchill calling at the Allied embassies to offer his congratulations. On both evenings there were fireworks and bonfires, singing and dancing in the streets—and always cheers. In the evening of May 9 the King broadcast from London to the rest of Britain and the Empire. "Let us remember," said His Majesty, " the men and women in all the Services who have laid down their lives . . . Let us salute in proud gratitude the great host of the living who have brought us to victory."

Sunday, May 13, was set aside as a National Day of Thanksgiving. At St. Paul's Cathedral the Royal Family, together with the leaders of the country and representatives of all the Allied governments, joined with ordinary men and women in a service conducted by the Archbishop of Canterbury. In other parts of the country ceremonial parades were combined with church services

5

LIGHTS OF VICTORY. *Crowds gathered outside Buckingham Palace on VE night. The floodlit building symbolized the triumph of light over the long darkness of war.*

CHEERS FOR THEIR MAJESTIES. *As the King and Queen toured the blitzed areas of London, people waved and cheered. This crowd demonstrated from a wrecked house.*

7

THUMBS UP. *On top of a car swarm some of the thousands who milled around London's West End. This was their day, the day of the ordinary people who had carried on.*

8

DANCING FOR JOY. *In Piccadilly Circus on VE Day great crowds abandoned them-selves to good-humoured rejoicing. Above is shown a group dancing the "Lambeth Walk."*

HOW AMERICA RECEIVED THE NEWS. *All over the United States, May 7 and 8 were commemorated by services of thanksgiving, processions and spontaneous public rejoicing. In New York great crowds gathered in Times Square, as shown in the above photograph. President Truman and his family attended the service held in Washington Cathedral. To the American people the President issued the following message: "This is a solemn and glorious hour. My only wish is that Franklin D. Roosevelt had lived to witness this day. General Eisenhower informs me that the forces of Germany have surrendered to the United Nations. The flags of freedom fly all over Europe. In this victory we join in offering our thanks to the Providence which has guided and sustained us through the dark days of our adversity. Our rejoicing is sober and subdued by the supreme consciousness of the terrible price we have paid to rid the world of Hitler and his evil band. Let us not forget, my fellow-Americans, the sorrow and heartbreak which abide today in the homes of so many of our neighbours—neighbours whose most priceless possession has been rendered as a sacrifice to redeem our liberty. We can repay the debt we owe to God, to our dead, and to our children only by work—ceaseless devotion to the responsibilities which lie ahead of us." President Truman also paid tribute to the "splendid contribution" of Britain and her Empire and the U.S.S.R. in the struggle.*

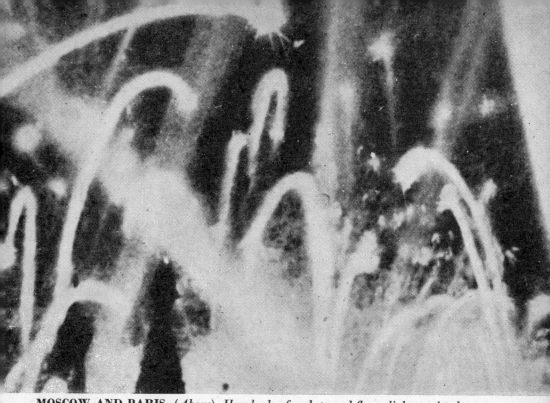

MOSCOW AND PARIS. (*Above*), *Hundreds of rockets and flares light up the sky over Moscow.* (*Below*), *VE Day crowds in Paris congregate round the Arc de Triomphe.*

THANKSGIVING. *St. Paul's, rising above bomb-scarred London, was the scene of a service of thanksgiving. Their Majesties are seen leaving St. Paul's in the Royal coach.*

LEADERS OF DEMOCRACY

THE free people of the world produced their own leaders in the fight against tyranny. They were appointed in democratic ways and supported by the united will of their people, whom they led to victory. They were statesmen, soldiers, scientists, trades unionists and industrialists— every sphere of human energy produced its men of the hour. And as the latent forces of democracy gathered strength and impetus it was proved for all time that efficiency and resource are not incompatible with freedom; that the self-discipline of proud and unfettered human beings is in the long run stronger than the regimentation of those who make one man their idol and worship the rule of force and the logic of total war. The men whose portraits are given in the following pages symbolize the united will of the peoples of the United Nations, and their personal sacrifices in the cause of freedom.

VITAL CONFERENCE.   *This photograph, taken at the Yalta meeting in February, 1945, shows Churchill, Roosevelt and Stalin with some of their principal advisers. This meeting completed the work of planning the final destruction of Hitler's Germany.*

MARSHAL STALIN. *After the death of Lenin, he emerged as the leader of Soviet Russia, and was largely responsible for the industrialization of his country. When Hitler suddenly attacked the U.S.S.R. Stalin planned the strategy that led the German armies to the debacle of Stalingrad and resulted in the fall of Berlin in May, 1945.*

FRANKLIN DELANO ROOSEVELT. *Four times President, he was one of the first to discern the evil ambitions of the Axis. Always willing to help the Allies during their time of mortal peril, he joined with Stalin and Churchill in planning Germany's defeat after Pearl Harbour in 1941. The President died suddenly on April 12, 1945.*

15

CHIANG KAI-SHEK. *President of China since 1943 and Chairman of the Supreme National Defence Council, he became the symbol of China's long defiance of Japan.*

CHARLES DE GAULLE. *When France fell, General de Gaulle led the Fighting French. After liberation of his country he became head of the Provisional Government in Paris.*

17

WAR CABINET WITH THE KING. *Above is shown the War Cabinet of Britain's All-Party Government, which was dissolved in May, 1945. (Left to Right), Mr. Herbert Morrison (Home Office, Home Security), Lord Woolton (Reconstruction), Sir John*

Anderson (Chancellor), Mr. C. R. Attlee (Deputy Prime Minister), H.M. the King,
Mr. Winston S. Churchill (Prime Minister), Mr. Anthony Eden (Foreign Affairs),
Mr. Oliver Lyttelton (Production) and Mr. Ernest Bevin (Labour and National Service).

19

PRESIDENT HARRY TRUMAN. *Following President Roosevelt's sudden death on April 12, 1945, Senator Harry S. Truman, who had been returned as vice-President in the elections held in the November of 1944, became President of the United States at the age of sixty-one. President Truman, who had made his reputation as head of the National Defence Investigation Committee, had been one of Missouri's representatives to Congress. He served with the American Army in France in the First World War.*

EMPIRE PRIME MINISTERS AND VICEROY. (*Top Left*), Mr. Peter Fraser, Labour Prime Minister of New Zealand; (*Top Right*), Mr. John Curtin, Labour Prime Minister of Australia; (*Bottom Left*), General Smuts, Prime Minister of South Africa; (*Bottom Right*), Mr. William Mackenzie King, Liberal Prime Minister of Canada; (*Centre*), Lord Wavell, appointed Viceroy of India in 1943.

GENERAL DWIGHT EISENHOWER. (*Above*), *Supreme Commander of the Allied Expeditionary Force in Western Europe. In 1942 President Roosevelt placed him in command of American forces in the European theatre of operations, and he demonstrated his great organizational ability and grasp of military strategy as Commander-in-Chief in Africa between 1942 and 1944. After final victory was won he was appointed American member of the Allied Control Council which ruled the defeated Germans.*

FIELD-MARSHAL SIR BERNARD MONTGOMERY. (*Right*), *given the command of the 8th Army in the field during the fighting in North Africa in October, 1942, Field-Marshal Montgomery consistently showed his ability to beat the best of the German commanders. After distinguishing himself still further in the Italian and Sicilian campaigns, he became Commander-in-Chief of the 21st Army group covering the northern sector of the Western Front. Received the capitulation of enemy troops in N.-W. Germany, and, after victory, was appointed British member of the Allied Control Council in Germany, together with Marshal Zhukov and General Eisenhower.*

SIR ARTHUR TEDDER. *Deputy Supreme Commander in Western Europe, Air Chief Marshal Tedder witnessed the Berlin capitulation for the Allied Expeditionary Force.*

SIR HENRY MAITLAND WILSON. *Leader of the British troops in the Greek campaign, Field Marshal Wilson became Senior British Military Representative in Washington.*

SIR ARTHUR HARRIS. *Officer-Commanding-in-Chief of Bomber Command, Air Marshal Harris directed the R.A.F. in its mighty blows against German war industries.*

FIELD-MARSHAL SIR HAROLD ALEXANDER. *Took command in Africa in 1942, and succeeded Field-Marshal Wilson as Supreme Commander in the Mediterranean.*

27

ADMIRAL LORD LOUIS MOUNTBATTEN. (*Above*), *Supreme Allied Commander in South-East Asia, the Admiral was formerly the Chief of Combined Operations.*

FIELD-MARSHAL SIR ALAN BROOKE. (*Right*), *Formerly Commander-in-Chief of the Home Forces, Sir Alan was appointed as Chief of the Imperial General Staff in 1941.*

SIR CHARLES PORTAL. (*Above*), *Marshal of the R.A.F. Sir Charles Portal became Chief of Air Staff in 1944. In this capacity he was one of the men responsible for the strategic bombing that partially destroyed the enemy's power to resist, the sinking of the great German battleships from the air, and the gigantic operations against flying bomb and rocket sites and communications centres on the Continent during that year.*

SIR ANDREW CUNNINGHAM. (*Left*), *First Sea Lord and Chief of Naval Staff since 1943, Sir Andrew was Naval Commander of the Allied Expeditionary Force to Africa in 1942, and, in 1943, C.-in-C. of the Mediterranean Allied Forces. In this capacity he planned the great task of transporting the men and material across the Mediterranean used in the successful invasions of Sicily and the Italian mainland.*

31

LAST BID FOR PEACE. *Mr. Neville Chamberlain returns to Britain after his meeting at Munich in 1938 with Hitler. He displays Hitler's signature on the agreement.*

PRELUDE TO WAR

POLAND in 1939 stood alone in the immediate path of the boundless ambition of Hitler and the great German war machine that had been built up in the years of the Nazi power.

Munich, which the civilized world prayed was the prelude to peace, was to prove the overture to the infernal drama of war. The plain fact was to emerge that the Axis used the promise of peace as an instrument with which to extract the utmost concessions from peace-loving nations before resorting to the double-edged weapon of force.

War of Nerves

During one uneasy year Britain and France, together with the great sister democracy of the United States and many smaller nations, watched the spectacle of Czecho-Slovakia being cynically pillaged and destroyed by the conquerors.

The figures of Hitler and Mussolini, now becoming increasingly disdainful of guarding their words and actions, were riveted in the spotlight of world news. Even the lesser men, the lieutenants of the robber chiefs, came in for their full share of publicity. Ribbentrop, smarting from an ingrained hatred of British institutions, and the boastful Count Ciano, son-in-law of the Duce, had staged a meeting at Salzburg on August 11—13. Again the world held its breath as these two figures were reported to have come to momentous decisions, keeping in constant touch with their respective bosses throughout the carefully staged conference.

The trend of events was soon to be made clear when the German Press started its clamour. "Danzig, the Polish Corridor, they must be returned to the Reich." This was the purport of dozens of leading articles and radio talks inside Nazi Germany. These were reflected in the columns of foreign newspapers, in Spain, Italy and the Balkans, that maintained close and not always reputable contact with the German Propaganda Ministry.

This war of words was repeating what had before taken place in respect of Czecho-Slovakia during 1938. First the demand for the redress of an "injustice" imposed by the Versailles Treaty; then the accounts of "atrocities" imposed on those of German blood.

It was clear that the issue was deeper than a mere territorial claim. Slow to make up its mind during the years of Nazi violence, power politics and racial persecution, the democratic world realized with a sudden, painful clarity that Hitler's policy was nothing short of world domination; that democracy and the Axis could not live together.

Poland's Valour

The Russo-German non-aggression pact, signed on August 23, with Ribbentrop as its proud architect, left Poland with no prospect of obtaining help in the East. France and Britain were resolved to make the issue one of principle—to cry "thus far and no farther" to the brown-shirted hordes. Yet, with her strong central position, Germany might strike before aid to her victim could be forthcoming.

Events tumbled swiftly towards the challenge. French, British and Polish military experts conferred: the shriek of atrocities was magnified in the Goebbels press.

Poland started to mobilize her 2,000,000 available reserves. Hitler decided to make his final effort.

PART ONE

BEFORE
FRANCE FELL

THE RAPE OF POLAND

ON August 24 the Anglo-Polish
Pact of mutual assistance was
signed: on August 31 Hitler issued
by radio a Sixteen-Point Demand to
Poland that would have virtually in-
corporated that country into the sphere
of Greater Germany. Quite typically the
Germans left no time for the Poles to
reply. Their tanks and forward units
rolled over the frontier: the Second
World War had begun.

With their comparatively old-
fashioned cavalry and infantry formations, their thin sprinkling of obsolescent aircraft and tanks, the Poles
were faced with the most scientifically
devised and compact weapon of war
that Germany's military genius could
devise: ten mechanized and motorized,
and forty-five infantry divisions, allied
to the then most powerful air force in
the world.

It was soon seen that the circumstances of war had completely changed
since the days of 1914-18. This was no
war between armies, but total war.
Advance troops of the Germans were
covered by aeroplanes, which blasted
great holes in the Polish air fields,
machine gunned and derailed trains
and supply columns, bombed and
demoralized the civilian population.
Parachute troops, first used by the
Russians, were landed behind the

WARSAW BURNS. *Virtually unopposed
in the skies, the Luftwaffe rained down
high explosive on the Polish capital.*

POLISH VILLAGERS LOSE THEIR HOMES. *Terror and destruction have come overnight to the scattered rural communities of Poland. A horse-drawn fire engine lumbers down the village street in a pathetic endeavour to quench the flames of war.*

Polish lines; sabotage by Nazi sympathizers could not be stopped. "The few aeroplanes Poland had for defence," said a Polish pilot, "were in the wider sense useless. But our pilots deliberately used their machines as projectiles and, sacrificing themselves, crashed purposely into the overwhelming masses of German machines."

Organized Massacre

As the series of enveloping pincer movements, planned to cut off and annihilate the various Polish groupings, operated with a clockwork precision, the full extent of German strength and heartlessness became apparent.

By September 4 they had captured and pillaged the towns of Katowice, Rybnik, Teschen and Frystat in Silesia, and the pincers crept forward upon

Warsaw. Hundreds of trains packed with civilian refugees were destroyed; German patrols searched for farmworkers, in the villages and fields, and methodically slaughtered them.

"I saw Lublin burned down on a plan," said a Polish doctor who survived the horror. "Children were impaled on the bayonets of drunken German soldiery, innocent men and women were shot in masses in the streets. German pilots, whose gloating faces could be seen, so low did they fly, came again and again to drop bombs in the middle of the crowded market place at Siedlce, sixty miles from Warsaw." Then came the turn of the capital.

Warsaw fought a hopeless fight for twenty-one days until the Military Governor was driven to surrender by the appalling sufferings of the civilian population who were being slowly exterminated by high explosives, hunger, thirst and disease.

As Warsaw burned, men and women fire-fighters battled all round the clock against the flames—battled till they fell by the side of their hoses and their machines. In the end there was no water and the fires were left to burn themselves out in the stricken city.

Bombed Hospitals

Mr. Drexel Biddle, United States Ambassador to Poland, has described how the Germans sought out the Warsaw hospitals and poured incendiary bombs on them.

"Many of our hospitals," said a refugee, "were crowded with choked and mutilated townspeople and soldiers. It became impossible to clear the dead from the wards or the streets. Hospitals and known centres of rest were marked by the German airmen and set ablaze. Columns of black smoke reared into the sky every day. Men and women of all walks of life would get their infirm and sick and what belongings they had and push them away in improvised carts. As they streamed off they were caught by bombers, artillery, or patrols and remorselessly wiped out. On one September day alone 3,000 Warsaw civilians were wiped out and dozens driven insane."

The surrender of Warsaw and the fall of Modlin came on September 28. Meanwhile Russia streamed over her border and effected a partition. Hitler had fulfilled his boast. Poland was no more except a vision held for the future by free men.

FLIGHT FROM THE TOWNS. *Their most prized possessions loaded on to handcarts, thousands of refugees from Polish towns take to the open country. Many of them were mowed down from the air, or butchered in cold blood by the advancing enemy troops.*

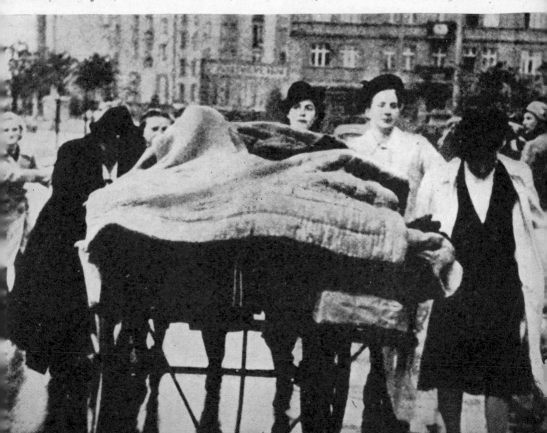

FIRST DAY OF WAR. *Crowds throng Whitehall on Sunday, September 3. Then the sudden wail of air-raid warnings sends them running to take cover in nearby shelters.*

BRITAIN DECLARES WAR

THE Munich crisis had come and gone in the autumn of 1938, leaving behind it the flickering embers of the international peace which had been kindled so auspiciously eighteen years before.

When the harvest had been gathered in and the full fruits of his Munich triumph picked by eager German hands, Hitler's controlled press began a fresh tirade of threats against Poland, a country whose frontiers were now guaranteed by Britain and France.

World Leaders Strive For Peace

Appalled at what they now saw so clearly, world leaders appealed to the German Leader, in the name of humanity, to pause for negotiated settlements. President Roosevelt, Mr. Mackenzie King (Prime Minister of Canada), the Pope, the Sovereigns of Holland and Belgium, all made urgent offers of mediation.

But on Friday, September 1, German troops invaded Poland while Allied diplomats were still seeking to establish some basis of rational discussion with the Master of Berchtesgaden.

Saturday, September 2, dawned warm and sunny, but filled with agonizing suspense for the people, anxious to know their fate. Scenes of the previous year were repeated—queues waited for gasmasks, crowds thronged Whitehall, sandbags and material for black-out became eagerly sought.

On the morning of Sunday, September 3, the nation was asked to stand by. A pronouncement was to be made at 11.15 a.m. by the Prime Minister, Mr. Neville Chamberlain. And when the appointed time arrived the tired and almost broken voice of the Prime Minister announced the declaration of war on Germany in these words, which were a disillusioned repudiation of the "appeasement" policy.

". . . Up to the very last it would have been quite possible to have arranged a peaceful and honourable settlement between Germany and Poland but Hitler would not have it. He had evidently made up his mind to attack Poland whatever happened and although he now says he put forward reasonable proposals that were rejected by the Poles, that is not a true statement. The proposals were never shown to the Poles nor to us, and, although they were announced in a German broadcast on Thursday night, Hitler did not wait to hear comments on them, but ordered his troops to cross the Polish frontier. His action shows convincingly that there is no chance of expecting that this man will ever give up his practice of using force to gain his will. He can only be stopped by force.

"We and France are to-day, in fulfilment of our obligations, going to the aid of Poland who is so bravely resisting this wicked and unprovoked attack on her people. We have a clear conscience. We have done all that any country could do to establish peace. The situation in which no word given by Germany's ruler could be trusted and no people or country could feel themselves safe was becoming intolerable and now that we have resolved to finish it I know that you will all play your part with calmness and courage.

"Now may God bless you all. May He defend the right. It is the evil things that we shall be fighting against, brute force, bad faith, injustice, oppression and persecution and against them I am certain that the right will prevail."

39

EXIT *GRAF SPEE*!

As the first wartime Christmas approached the first big story of success sent a thrill of hope through the hearts of the Allies.

It was the story of the sinking of the *Admiral Graf Spee*. This 10,000 ton German pocket battleship had acted as a commerce raider on the open seas since the outbreak of war. In her were 62 survivors of nine British merchant ships she had destroyed.

On December 14, 1939, the now immortal British light cruisers, *Achilles* (7,000 tons), *Ajax* (7,000 tons), and *Exeter* (8,300 tons), intercepted *Admiral Graf Spee*, whose armament was superior to the total of all three of them. On any mathematical reckoning the little British ships should have turned away, but, on the "Nelson" reckoning, they nosed in and about for a fight, defying the 11in. guns of the Germans.

Exeter was badly mauled early. "Our steering gear soon went," said a British sailor, "but we stuck it. Ten of us got in a line and handed on orders from the bridge to the aft steering wheel as we limped about still pumping shot

from our one remaining 8in. gun. We handed ammunition about in a chain like that too."

Not until she was crippled did *Exeter* fall out of the line. By this time Commodore Henry Harwood (now Admiral Sir Henry) had manœuvred his ships at superior speed and had so bewildered and punished the big German that her Commander, Captain Hans Langsdorff raced for sanctuary in the harbour at Montevideo. Turned out after 72 hours Langsdorff, afraid to face the British force waiting for him, scuttled his ship in the Estuary of the River Plate and on December 20 committed suicide at Buenos Aires. His crew, who were reported to have shown signs of mutiny in the closing stages of the battle, were interned by the Argentine Government.

Seen above is a photograph showing the last moments of the doomed ship. Ablaze in all parts, and listing heavily, she is wreathed in a pall of smoke as she settles for her death plunge beneath the Atlantic waters.

Said the *New York Times* next day: "The *Graf Spee* fought only one battle and she ran away from that one."

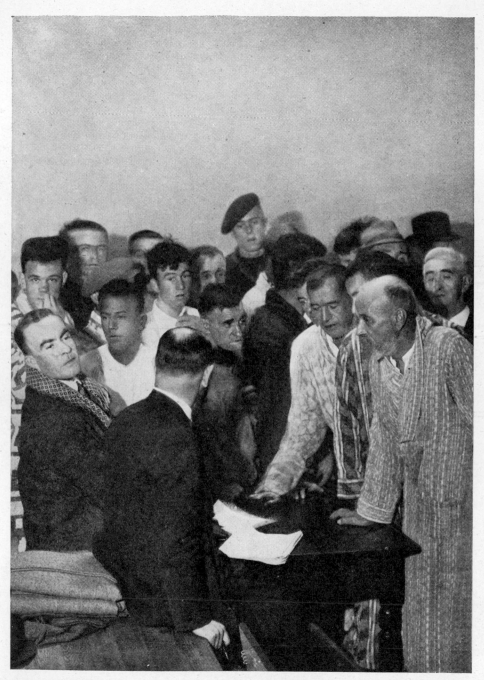

BACK TO FREEDOM. *Here are some of the men who were to have provided a Nazi triumph. Soon after their release from Altmark, H.M.S. Cossack landed them in a British port.*

THE *ALTMARK* INCIDENT

THE amazing story of *Altmark* which opens far out in the south-western Atlantic and arrives at its thrilling climax on the coast of Norway, more than 12,000 miles away, is a sequel to the story of *Graf Spee*.

Altmark, under the command of Captain Dahl, was a large oil-tanker disguised as a Norwegian merchant ship. On her bows and stern was painted the name *Sogne Oslo*. She was companion tender to *Graf Spee* and had halted on December 6 to take more captured merchant seamen aboard from the German raider. This consignment sent *Altmark's* captive complement up to 300 officers and men. Captain Dahl had a fanatical hatred of all things British; he vented this to the full on the hapless captives, existing on starvation rations, in the badly ventilated bowels of the ship.

Germany Prepares to Celebrate

It must have been a bad hour for the gallant captain when he received news of the disaster to *Graf Spee*. What was he to do, stationed as he was without his supporting leader, and with the British blockade remorselessly stretching between himself and Germany?

He decided to run the blockade.

Early in February, 1940, he was on the North Atlantic trade route; by mid-February he reached Norwegian waters near the Trondheim Fiord.

Norwegian patrols examined him. *Altmark* was clearly a war vessel, but Dahl was allowed to proceed. He cautiously nosed his vessel down the coast under the protection of the neutral zone.

The British Navy watched. Germany made great preparations to welcome Dahl and his band of British prisoners.

"We knew vaguely what was going on," said one of them later. "We knew well that a Norwegian officer had come along and we all banged the ship's plates and shouted like hell and blew whistles. We cheered and sang and groaned and howled — but the Norwegian officer made no sign."

"Stop the prison ship!"

British aeroplanes quickly spotted *Altmark*. From the Admiralty the order went out and instantly the cruiser *Arethusa* and the destroyers *Cossack* and *Enterprise* went in. They found *Altmark* on February 17 steaming with the Norwegian torpedo boat *Kjell* at her side. Dahl ignored the signalled order to change course and the warning shot that followed. Off he ran for shelter through the ice of Joessing Fiord.

Captain Vian of *Cossack* gave the Norwegians an opportunity to follow up the Fiord with him to make enquiries. They declined and so Vian went alone. Like a man who meant it he morsed to *Altmark*: "Turn about or I open fire on you."

Dahl then ran *Altmark* aground.

The Navy's Here

Vian put his destroyer alongside.

Lieut.-Commander Bradwell T. Turner was first over on the *Altmark* poop. Two officers and thirty men with revolvers, rifles, and bayonets followed him. After a sharp hand to hand fight, in which seven Germans were killed, they were masters of the ship,

The prisoners below fought for places at their peep holes. Their hearts were pounding with excitement and hope.

Doors were crashed down. A hearty voice called, "Are you British prisoners?"

"Yes," they cried.

"Then you're safe: the Navy's here."

DENMARK INVADED

"**B**RITAIN,**" observed Hitler in the
early days of 1940, "has begun
her war against the neutral
world by measures of hunger blockade.
She has dealt a murderous blow at the
concept of neutrality itself."

At dawn on April 9, 1940, Germans
disembarked at Copenhagen after being
ferried across the Baltic. Motorized
units stormed across the narrow land
frontier in the South. Hitler's pronouncement was brief and to the point:

"No Englishman," he shouted, "shall
show his nose in Norway or Denmark
for the rest of the war."

Thousands of Danes learned the
news as they cycled to work, powerless
and bewildered workmen found themselves surrounded by the invading
troops. German marching songs echoed
through the streets.

It was nearly a bloodless victory. Let
a Dane who escaped to Allied territory
tell the story:

"Some of us started to resist. There
was more than one street fight but it
was soon over because King Christian
explained on the air that resistance
would be hopeless and that the German
occupation had been accepted by the
Danish Government under protest."

Herr Stauning, Danish Prime
Minister, broadcast an appeal to the
Danish people, urging them to adopt a
"correct" attitude to the German
troops who had been sent to occupy
the country. Any resistance was useless.

Within a few hours all communication with the outside world was
cut off. Denmark was overhung by the
Nazi darkness and her free institutions
were progressively smothered.

FRUITS OF VICTORY. *In the streets of
captured Copenhagen Nazi Storm Troops
load lorries with "commandeered" plunder.*

NORWAY FALLS TO HITLER

O<small>N</small> April 9, 1940, aided by traitors led by Major Quisling, the Nazis seized Oslo. Called to surrender, King Haakon refused to have any dealings with the Nazis.

On April 14, British naval forces landed at Namsos, followed by a hastily organized expeditionary force. There followed a difficult campaign, at the end of which the Allies were forced to withdraw. King Haakon and his Government came to England with many Norwegian soldiers, airmen and sailors who continued the fight.

Perhaps the most heartening element in the campaign was the work of the British Navy at the "iron ore" port of Narvik.

Crack modern destroyers, units of the German Navy, sneaked up the sixty miles of fiord and established themselves in the key port. Artillery pieces were rapidly improvised on the shore to command the waterway against attack.

Destroyers Dash in

Captain Warburton - Lee, having been given permission to decide for himself whether or not to attack, went with his five destroyers up the narrow mine-strewn waters. He and his men made a fight that Mr. Churchill described as being "equal in daring and brilliance to anything in the long annals of the Royal Navy."

Six German destroyers of the latest and largest type were found in the lair as well as a formidable array of shore batteries and guns.

But the little British destroyers ran the gauntlet and made their challenge. They put a 1,600 ton German to the bottom, left three more heavily hit and burning, and sank six merchant vessels, as they battered their way on.

"There was hell while it lasted," said a British seaman afterwards. "It was give and take at close quarters with little room for tricks and evasions. *Hunter* first absorbed punishment and went down fighting. Anyway we left the 'Jerry' boats in a mess. *Hardy* was so severely damaged that she had to run ashore. *Hotspur* was badly crippled. She got away covered by *Hostile* and *Havoc*."

Captain Warburton-Lee was killed in the heat of the action: his posthumous V.C. ranks high among the deeds of bravery.

Then came a grand sequel. On the way out through the fiord the battle-scarred British ships met the big German ship *Rauensfeld* packed with supplies and joyously sank her.

After this glorious adventure the Second Destroyer Flotilla blockaded the enemy in Narvik Fiord. Then, on April 13, *Warspite*, with Vice-Admiral Whitworth in command, led a force of destroyers and mine-sweeping appliances up the fiord to a new attack.

H.M.S. *Cossack* put a shore field howitzer out of action; when the smoke cleared four German destroyers were shattered and sunk in Narvik Bay.

Three others fled up Rombaks Fiord, a small inlet eight miles long behind Narvik town. After a running fight and chase these, too, were destroyed.

"Norwegians cried for Joy"

"Those of us who saw the fighting in the narrow Narvik waters will never forget it," said a petty officer who was in *Warspite*. "The flashing guns showed vividly on the background of snow, and the booming of explosives echoed weirdly about the lovely hills."

SMOKE OF BATTLE. *Extent of the destruction in Narvik Bay after the attacks by British warships. Burning ships and buildings are an awe-inspiring background.*

CHURCHILL PRIME MINISTER

IT is May, 1940. The unnatural lull which prevailed through the winter is over. The fury of mechanized warfare has been unleashed.

The people of Britain gather round wireless sets waiting tensely for each news bulletin. Newspapers are sold out soon after editions reach the streets. The public mood is wondering and uneasy, for the Germans have seized Norway and Denmark.

The People's Will.

Neville Chamberlain, the Prime Minister, has told a restless House of Commons the story of Allied failure in Norway. At the end of his speech a Division has been taken and the small Government majority of 81 makes it clear that his period of office is at an end.

In the headlines and over the wireless comes news of Chamberlain's resignation and of a new Prime Minister, Winston Churchill. In tired tones the defeated Leader of the House makes his farewell address to the nation.

Then the evening of May 10. Already the crowds in Whitehall know the news. German panzers are pouring through the Low Countries, French and British divisions are moving up into Belgium. Memories of 1914 become vivid.

Meanwhile Churchill has formed his new Cabinet—a coalition of Conservatives, Labour, and Liberals.

As dusk fell on that perfect spring day the thoughts of citizens of towns, villages and hamlets centre on the British fighting men who, separated by a narrow stretch of water, oppose a Nazi army of unknown strength. In

GRIM DAYS AHEAD. *As he pauses on the steps of* 10 *Downing Street, Mr. Churchill's face is stern and anxious.*

spite of the soporific effect of months of confidence in the Maginot Line and the Allied Blockade a foreboding of greater reverses is abroad.

While the German drive pressed on towards Northern France Mr. Churchill rises in the House on May 13 to move the resolution welcoming the new Government as representing the united will of the nation to see the war to a victorious conclusion. He speaks these solemn words :

"I would say to the House as I said to those who have joined the Government, 'I have nothing to offer but blood, toil, tears and sweat.' We have before us an ordeal of a most grievous kind, we have before us many many long months of struggle and suffering. You ask what is our policy. I will say it is to wage war by land, sea and air with all our might and all the strength that God can give us, and to wage war against a monstrous tyranny never surpassed in the dark lamentable catalogue of human crime. That is our policy."

The Nation Speaks.

Mr. Churchill's motion is seconded by Mr. H. B. Lees-Smith on behalf of the Labour Party. In that hour of dreadful peril, more dreadful than the men and women of this country know, there is no thought of party opportunism, no desire to make political capital of disaster. There remains only the determination to see things through come what may, until the bitter end.

So the vote on the resolution is carried by 381 votes to none against.

And in the factories and homes of Britain the Voice of the Commons is amplified a million times as the men and women of Britain find themselves face to face with the realities of war.

BELGIUM AGAIN!

IN these early days of May the available trained man-power of France and Britain is waiting in Northern France. It seems as if the stalemate may continue indefinitely. The papers show pictures of front-line concerts, football matches "somewhere in France." It is the heyday of the Maginot Line, General Gamelin (the man who knows how to win by waiting), Reynaud (the strong man of France), and stories and rumours of impending German shortages.

Belgium and Holland have clung desperately to their neutrality, an attitude which is understandable but which ignores two basic facts—the unscrupulousness of the Nazi power-mongers and the strategic possibility of turning the Maginot defences by a thrust through the Low Countries.

With suddenness on May 10 the news flashes to the world that Belgium and Holland are attacked by Germany. A call to the Allies comes from Belgium's young King Leopold. French and British troops move up into Belgium. It is 1914 all over again. Our troops receive a tumultuous welcome from the brave little nation who shared the horrors of 1914-18.

The Belgians are already involved in heavy fighting at the vital Albert Canal and the River Meuse, and in the Ardennes. The might of the Luftwaffe is unleashed over Alost, Louvain, Renaix and Brussels. It is said that at least 2,000 German heavy tanks are in the fighting about Liége.

Against this mailed punch to the heart the Allies can only muster forces which are inferior in modern armaments to the enemy. The Germans have planned and timed their offensive well, aided by the strict neutrality of

BRUGES CAPTURED. *Tramping Nazi jackboots ring on the cobbled city streets.*

their Dutch and Belgian victims who only now are entering into close military collaboration with the Allies.

"Hitler," says the concerted voice of outraged American opinion, "has added one more disgrace to his detested

*The day is May 28, 1940. Bruges is only one of many Belgian cities that have fallen
to the Germans as King Leopold announces that the Belgian army has had to surrender.*

name, one more to his lengthening
list of horrible crimes."

But as yet decent men are not armed
and trained on a scale to overpower
the wild beast, who is machine-
gunning refugees, slowly paralysing
unprotected cities from the air. Then
comes the paralysing shock.

On May 28 King Leopold has to
announce that Belgian resistance is at
an end. The Belgian Government is
reported to have arrived in Paris.

51

GERMAN LESSON. *Walls of the Grosse Kerk, the principal church of Rotterdam, are all that remain standing for a square mile in the heart of the historic Dutch city. For three hours it had been mercilessly bombed, totally without anti-aircraft protection.*

The Germans deliberately sent over wave after wave of bombers to destroy one of the most densely populated districts as a demonstration of Nazi terror. Two hospitals and the town hall, as well as most of the main shopping centre, were razed to the ground.

53

AMSTERDAM'S TURN. *It is May 10, 1940. The shriek of bombers diving out of the sun has heralded the worst raid on Holland's capital. Huge clouds of smoke indicate the fearful destruction inflicted on thousands of small homes in a residential district.*

HOLLAND'S HEROISM

SINCE Napoleon set forth on his bitter journey from the field of Waterloo to exile on St. Helena, the history of Holland, ruled by the House of Orange, had been one of peace, broken only by one military campaign of short duration. In the First World War she had preserved her neutrality. Her statesmen were confident that they could keep neutral in the Second and greater war.

Where the Kaiser had at least forborne to strike, the new master of the Reich possessed no scruple. Hypocritical words of friendship poured forth from Nazi diplomats, but at the German War Office hard-faced Junker officers drew up plans for invasion. And on May 10 the calm of the Dutch countryside was broken by the shrill whine of dive bombers hurtling out of the sun, the roar of tanks and mechanized columns.

Studied Brutality

First aircraft, then tanks and infantry; the merciless bombing of civilians, the encirclement of a small and weakly equipped army. This was the trusted military recipe applied with cold and studied brutality by the German High Command.

To their eternal credit, the Dutch authorities, hopelessly outnumbered in men, deficient in all varieties of arms, decided to fight. They flung their available manpower to the line of Ijsel and Maas (Meuse). They carried out demolitions, resorted to Holland's traditional defence of opening the dykes and allowing the water to sweep over rich agricultural land.

It was David versus Goliath—a Goliath fortified by armour plate.

German paratroops showered down on the countryside to confuse and terrify the population with sabotage and killing. The tragic reality of the Nazi mastery of the Fifth Column, basest of the brutal arts, became vivid. In Rotterdam, in Delft, at the Hague, Dutch - Germans, "tourists," and "refugees" planted by the Nazis in readiness, were trained and rehearsed. Thousands of disguised German troops had been hiding in Dutch barges for days. Fifth Columnists and arriving paratroops knew where to go, and the precise whereabouts of military objectives.

Rescue of the Royal Family

Soon the enemy were in control of the big aerodromes, including those at Rotterdam and the Hague. Their attempt to capture Queen Wilhelmina and her Government at Scheveningen failed. The royal party were taken off by British destroyer to England.

British airmen flew hundreds of sorties to help. British vessels shelled German concentrations about the Dutch coast. Meanwhile Dutch soldiers fought for their country with desperate valour—their little air force of 200 machines brought down far more than 200 of the enemy's, but by May 14 the Dutch forces had lost 100,000 men.

The casualty list of civilians and fighting men was assuming horrifying proportions. It was with this in mind that the small nation, having proved its manhood to the full in battle, laid down its arms.

"On the evening of May 14 we gave in," said General Winkelman, Dutch C.-in-C. "The superiority of the modern weapons held by the enemy left us with no chance and the massacre of civilian townsmen and refugees made further resistance impossible."

STAGES OF GERMAN ADVANCE. *Outlined above are stages of the German drive, culminating in the evacuation of Dunkirk and the loss of all France north of the Somme. The intention of the Allied High Command had been to close the gap created by the German break through at Sedan and across the River Maas until reinforcements of men and material could be brought up. When this failed, and the Belgian Army ceased to exist as a fighting force, the enemy, in Mr. Churchill's vivid phrase, "swept like a scythe around the right and rear of the Armies of the North." Only retreat remained.*

For the time being all available German strength was utilized in an effort to seal off the British from the coast, after which they would have been slowly annihilated. At one time it seemed quite impossible that any large number of Allied troops could reach Dunkirk. That the ever-narrowing corridor within which the British and French armies fought was still kept open was due to the heroism shown by men who kept hitting back when all hope seemed gone. Notable episodes were the defence of Boulogne by the Guards and the last stand at Calais. Study of dates given will show how narrowly disaster was averted.

THE EPIC OF DUNKIRK

In the days between May 27 and June 3 watchers on the Kentish coast saw a strange activity in the Channel. Making their way towards France were destroyers and other units of the Royal Navy; merchant vessels, large and small; plodding colliers and coastal tramps; fishing vessels, their decks still spattered with gleaming scales; paddle steamers that once gave thousands of holiday-makers in paper hats a brief taste of life afloat; a London Fire Brigade float, the *Massey Shaw;* yachts ranging from the playthings of millionaires to humble week-enders; frail dinghies towed by motor launch.

They came back, did most of the 2,000 vessels of this motley armada, with their decks crammed with unshaven, weary men of the British Expeditionary Force and French and Belgian armies, 335,000 of them snatched from the closing jaws of the rapidly advancing Nazi armies.

RIFLES VERSUS DIVE-BOMBERS. *On the beaches at Dunkirk men of the retreating British Forces pit their rifles against the constantly attacking Luftwaffe.*

Behind this lay an almost incredible story of heroism and resource.

With the collapse of organized Belgian resistance, Lord Gort had ordered a retreat of the B.E.F. towards Dunkirk. The road to Amiens and the south was blocked by enemy units.

Germany Closes the Trap

General Weygand, who had assumed command of the French armies, planned, in the words of Mr. Churchill, for the French and British troops in Belgium—"to keep on holding the right hand of the Belgians and to give their own right hand to the newly created French army, which was to have advanced across the Somme in great strength to grasp it."

This plan did not materialize. Shattered by tanks and dive-bombers, the Belgian army had virtually ceased to exist as a fighting force: communications between the French and British in Belgium and the main French forces were beyond all possible repair.

The French massed to defend a hastily constructed line running south of the Somme and the Aisne and linking up with the Maginot Line. For

Explosions out to sea and ominous smoke clouds mark the steadily increasing pressure from the enemy; only faith and great courage stand between an army and defeat.

the troops in Belgium only a faint hope of rescue by sea remained.

Never did the time factor assume so much importance. Four thousand men —the Queen Victoria Rifles, the Rifle Brigade, the 60th Rifles, a battalion of British tanks, and one thousand Frenchmen—pushed their way into Calais in a desperate attempt to win a few hours for their brothers in the north.

They fought with cold, reasoned bravery, pitting their lives against the infuriated hammer blows rained upon them by the enemy, while the hands of the clock marked each minute and hour so hardly won. Tanks were turned into fortresses, rifles used against tommy guns. Only 30 survivors of the gallant 4,000 were eventually taken off by the Royal Navy on May 26.

Meanwhile hell raged on the sand dunes and pier of the port of Dunkirk, so familiar to tourists in the palmy days of peace. Dog-tired troops continued to pile up. They were battered continually by the German artillery as it crept remorselessly forward; their eardrums ceaselessly assailed by the wail of diving German planes and the whistle and explosion of bombs.

"Where is the R.A.F.?"

The Royal Air Force, outnumbered but never outfought, flung everything they had into the sky. The pilots, red-eyed from lack of sleep, grimy, and in many cases wounded, were in action as many as sixteen hours each day. One squadron of 12 two-seater all-metal Defiants accounted for fifty enemy aircraft in three days.

Yet British planes were pitifully few compared with the seemingly inexhaustible resources of the Luftwaffe.

MAIN STREET. *Masses of wrecked equipment flank Dunkirk's shattered houses as the evacuation from the beaches is completed.*

Some of the patiently-waiting men on the beaches saw nothing but swarms of Nazi aircraft. "Where is the R.A.F.?" they asked. The answer was that the R.A.F. had to make the best of scanty reserves. Not only were many enemy machines intercepted and prevented from ever reaching Dunkirk, but the German army was impeded by the constant, daring, low-level attacks made upon gun emplacements, troop columns and rear positions.

As the battle, openly heralded in Berlin as one of extermination, was reaching its climax, the evacuation was being planned by grave-faced men in a small room let into the cliffs of Dover.

Churchill Warns Parliament

At first it seemed merely a question of rescuing a small percentage. Churchill warned an awed House of Commons "to prepare itself for hard and heavy tidings." The German High Command felt confident enough to announce : "The ring about the British, French, and Belgian armies is closed for ever." They forgot Britain's traditional ally—the sea.

From Whitehall the call went out for ships and the men to man them. It was heard in the offices of shipping lines and trawling companies; in clubs and factories; it echoed through the narrow streets of ports and small fishing towns. The men and the ships were forthcoming. Red tape was cut as only democracy can cut it in emergency.

It is now no secret that expert opinion budgeted for at most 30,000 men to be taken off. The difficulties which had to be faced were frankly incredible. One factor, heaven sent, was in favour of the rescuers—a sudden calm descended on the Channel, enabling operations to be carried out that would have been impossible in rough weather.

DUNKIRK BEACH-HEAD. *Drawn up in long, winding lines, British troops preserve perfect discipline as they patiently await their turn to be taken off the beaches.*

No attempt was made by the Germans to cut off the British forces by sea otherwise than by mines and shore batteries—the main route had to be altered three times because of these—and by air attack.

Dunkirk is set in a coastline riddled by shoals, sandbanks and narrow passages, hazards that were increased as most of the rescue work had to be done at night. Moreover, owing to the shallow water, ships larger than destroyers were prevented from reaching the pier.

The scene was unforgettable. Against an inferno of bursting high explosive, troops waded out to small boats and rafts that carried them to the waiting rescue vessels. It was a nightmare for the wounded. Rescue parties of stout-hearted and strong-backed sailors carried them on board. The devil's chorus of guns, bullets, and bombs grew greater every passing hour. The reverberations could be heard from the English coast, where watchers strained their eyes to catch each ominous flash on the horizon.

Then the news broke to the world: 335,000 men rescued, British casualties throughout the campaign, "exceeding 30,000 killed, missing and wounded."

Uncomplainingly the wounded lie ready to be carried through the surf to the ships; each hour brings fresh contingents of weary men to the already over-crowded beaches.

At south-eastern ports the whole population turned out to welcome back the men from Dunkirk. The Churches, the Salvation Army, the W.V.S. and many other organizations had piles of food and hot tea ready. There were gifts of cigarettes and of chocolate. Crowds cheered them off from railway stations. Union Jacks fluttered, together with hastily improvised banners bearing words like "Bravo, B.E.F." and "Welcome Home." Weary as they were, many of the men contrived a cheery smile and an exchange of badinage as they saw their welcome.

The free world hailed the evacuation as a victory for freedom. And victory it was, compared with the disaster which had been so narrowly averted.

World Comment.

Typical was a comment in the *New York Times:* "So long as the English tongue survives, the word Dunkerque will be spoken with reverence. For in that harbour, in such a hell as never blazed on earth before, at the end of a lost battle, the rags and blemishes that have hidden the soul of democracy fell away. There, beaten but unconquered, in shining splendour, she faced the enemy."

HOME ! *Into harbour, packed with ships of all sizes and types, steam the transports from Dunkirk. Emergency feeding canteens for thousands of men have been improvised.*

The wounded were rushed to emergency hospitals; special trains carried tired, grimy men through Southern England. It was an hour of deadly danger and deep thankfulness.

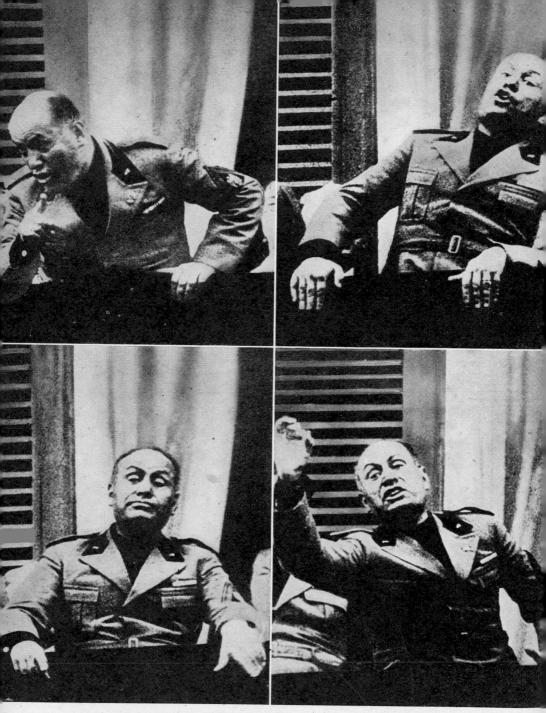

"I HAVE WAITED FOR THIS HOUR." *These four studies of Benito Mussolini show his elation at the German victories in France, his eager anticipation of an easy share in the spoils of war as he hurriedly declares that henceforth Italy will fight alongside Nazi Germany against the Democracies, whom he now thinks are doomed.*

ITALY ENTERS THE WAR

Hot sunlight blazes down on to the historic city of Rome. It is June 10, 1940, and a suppressed excitement makes the sultry air more oppressive. Before the resplendent Palazzo Venezia there is a milling throng. Fascists strut in uniform, policemen marshal the crowds, plain clothes detectives and spies of Mussolini's Ovra, the feared secret police, mingle with the perspiring throng of civilians and military.

Hour of Triumph

A momentary hush, then roars of applause as the cheer-leaders get to work, and out on to the balcony comes Benito Mussolini. Up and out goes the much photographed chin, the hand is raised in the Fascist salute, and he bellows to the crowd below that the die is irretrievably cast. To the accompaniment of hysterical cheering, from the younger members of his audience at least, the Italian dictator achieves his most grandiose moment of triumph: "It is," he shouts, "the struggle of fruitful, young people against sterile people on the threshold of their decline." The cameras click, the uniforms make a gay sight in the sunlight. The first act of the Italian tragedy has begun.

Mussolini's son-in-law, Count Ciano, had enjoyed his moment in the lime-light as, with an arrogant gesture, he handed Italy's declaration of war to the British and French ambassadors. Military bands marched and remarched through the streets. Triumphal arches erected by Roman emperors looked down upon the black-shirted Italian youths who cried, "Nice, Corsica, Tunis, Suez." Easy dividends, prospects of the fleshpots to be provided by the cheaply bought new

Roman Empire, made a rich banquet that the Italian people, with their flair for pageantry, enjoyed upon that June day.

For nine months Italy's attitude of non-belligerency and the inspired denunciations in the controlled Italian puppet press had tied down a French army in the south, French and British forces in Africa, and impelled the Allies to strengthen their Mediterranean naval units.

Now those who had prophesied that the Fascists were only waiting the most favourable opportunity to make a bid for territorial aggrandizement found themselves justified by events.

From the other side of the Brenner Pass, the senior partner in the Axis, Adolf Hitler, telegraphed that he was deeply moved by Mussolini's historic decision, and assured the Duce and King Victor Emmanuel of Germany's "indivisible community" in the struggle that was to come.

What it meant to the Allies

The entry of Italy into the arena was a heavy blow to the Allies, labouring under the full force of the successful German onslaught in the North. It meant that Hitler, already enjoying the advantage in aircraft and tanks, was reinforced by a large navy—fifth in the list regarding world strength; an army which, despite weaknesses it had shown in the Spanish Civil War, was numerically equal to that of Great Britain, and an air force of about 1,500 machines. It meant that the Suez Canal was imperilled and our main line of communication with India and the East put in jeopardy by the large, well-equipped Italian armies standing ready in North Africa.

ITALY MARCHES. *Italian mountain troops, equipped with skis, wend their way across the Alps after Mussolini's declaration of war against the Allies. There was little fighting in this campaign, which ended in the Italian-French Armistice of June 25.*

Although the Duce's army occupied Mentone, on the French Riviera, the Germans did not allow their ally to seize much French territory. All Italy obtained from her treachery was a cheap triumph and the opportunity of fighting the British Forces in Africa.

CAPITULATION OF FRANCE

WHEN Mussolini threw off the mask and announced that Italy would henceforth fight side by side with Germany, there came an immediate reaction from an already desperate France.

Prime Minister Reynaud made his final, despairing signal for help. To President Roosevelt he sent the following appeal on June 10, when the French Government were going to Tours: "For six days and nights our armies have been fighting an enemy with crushing material superiority. The Hun is almost at the gates of Paris. But we shall fight behind Paris, we shall shut ourselves up in one of our provinces, and if they drive us out of that we shall go to North Africa. I beg of you to help us before it is too late."

Across the Atlantic, as the world drama unfolded tragedy upon tragedy, came the President's reply: "We will extend to the opponents of force the material resources of this nation." But by June 14 the French armies had abandoned Paris. German troops marched through the deserted streets: the Swastika flew at the pinnacle of the Eiffel Tower.

Churchill in Paris

Not many hours before, Winston Churchill had been in the French capital striving like a colossus to save some of the crumbling foundations of Western civilization. He offered to France a solemn pact of union between the two countries. It provided that France and Great Britain should no longer be two nations. There would be indissoluble union, and during the war a single war cabinet. On each side citizens would enjoy joint citizenship. By a small majority the French cabinet declined the offer.

Words of encouragement poured over the air from Britain. Out of its

FORGING CHAINS FOR FRANCE. *German and French representatives walk towards the railway coach in which Hitler's armistice terms are to be read and accepted.*

GANGSTERS IN CONFERENCE. *Waiting the arrival of the French are, right to left, Brauchitsch, Raeder (half-hidden), Hitler, Hess, Goering, Keitel and Ribbentrop.*

depleted resources the British Government promised reinforcements of men and weapons. "We will face the ordeal of fire together—we shall not turn from the conflict until France stands erect once more in her grandeur. Nothing will deter our faith that France will rise again." So said the British message.

Petain Takes Over

By June 16 Paul Reynaud had failed and a Government was formed by Marshal Pétain.

Eagerly, anxiously, all Britain, all the outside world, waited for news. What would Pétain do? Would French forces continue the fight in the south of France, and from North Africa if need be?

Then, on June 17, the decision came from the aged Marshal. He had, he said, watched with horror the distress of French refugees from the battle zone. "It is with a heavy heart that I tell you we must cease to fight. I have applied to our opponent to ask if he is ready to sign an armistice with us as between soldiers after fighting—and in honour." The words came over the air at noon to stun the minds of millions of listeners in Britain and the U.S.A.

Swiftly the Germans tightened their hold on France. They advanced to the centre and the south. Then Hitler took a melodramatic revenge. In the Forest of Compiègne, on the same spot and in the same railway coach in which Foch dictated the Armistice to Germany 22 years before, the terms imposed by Germany were read out by General Keitel in the presence of Hitler, Goering, Hess, Ribbentrop, Admiral Raeder and the French plenipotentiaries.

The day was June 22. France accepted the German terms "under the compulsion of military events," and Keitel, smiling cynically in the interior of the stuffy railway coach, said: "As a soldier I have only to add that we know how to honour the defeat of a courageous foe."

71

THE HEART OF FRANCE. *Crack German troops on horseback parade through the streets of Paris for the second time in history, arrogant and flushed with easy victory.*

In the background of the photograph is the *Arc de Triomphe*, erected to celebrate *French* victories won by Napoleon, where the grave of *France's* Unknown Warrior reposes.

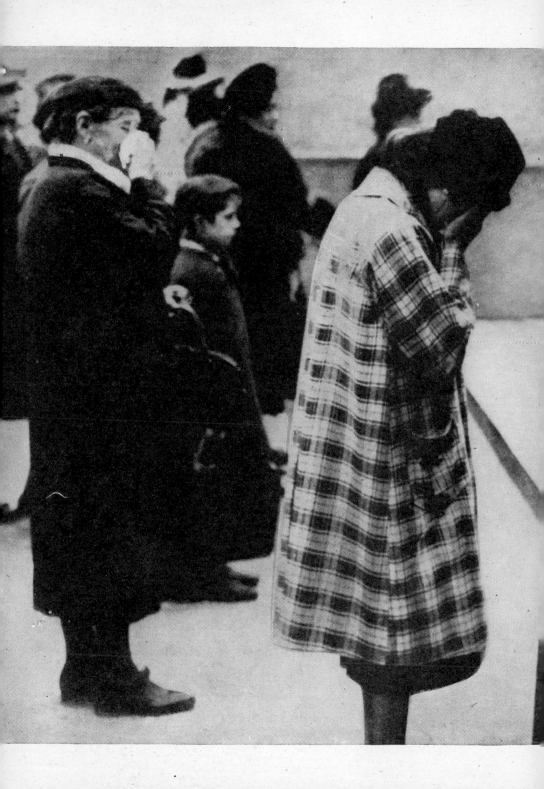

FRANCE IN CHAINS

"I SAW Frenchmen and French-women wandering about country lanes on the outskirts of Paris for days after the surrender. Some of them searched for lost relatives, but all were dazed and many of them dumb and speechless through shock."

These were the words of one who escaped from the French crash to Britain. He continued the ghastly story of ruthless massacre thus :

"As the armies fell back I saw whole families machine-gunned and wiped out on the roadside. German tanks were deliberately run over masses of people in flight. Our village, twenty-five miles from Paris, was made a sporting target by German dive bombers. Slowly and methodically they slaughtered a huddled crowd of old people and terrified children.

"It was pathetic to see simple country folk trying to rescue some of their personal belongings and their pet animals," said an escaped French officer. "There were on the roads about the old battlefields and near Paris ragged battalions made up of civilians and soldiers alike. But although their leader had surrendered and although they were caught in a trap the French people had clearly not surrendered in their hearts. They knew without knowing, in their misery, that some day liberation would come—that Free France could not die."

General de Gaulle, one of France's most brilliant younger generals, arrived in Britain to place himself at the disposal of the Allies as representative of the Fighting French, who still had faith in ultimate victory.

BITTER REMEMBRANCE. *These French women weep before the Memorial to the Dead of 1914–18 at Bordeaux.*

PART TWO

BRITAIN STANDS FIRM

DEMOCRACY AT BAY

THE incredible had become history. Britain stood alone on the one bridgehead of western civilization. Across the Channel the German armies were consolidating their conquests. Hitler and his staff looked across the narrow expanse of water and considered the best way of subduing the small islands that rashly stood between Germany and the domination of western Europe.

It seemed absurd by German reckoning that Great Britain, with her forty-six million people, would continue to fight. The enemy's broadcasting stations poured forth a mixture of cajolery and threats. German propagandists invented the myth of a half-starving British populace clamouring for peace at any price.

But in the islands themselves a moral calm prevailed that astounded foreign observers. It was almost as though centuries of tradition inspired the British people with the inherent belief that their country had not attained a glorious destiny to become enslaved by the Nazis.

Winston Churchill was voicing the sentiments of the silent millions of his countrymen when he announced Britain's determination to fight on. Without heroics Democracy rolled up its sleeves and went to its action stations.

TOWER OF LONDON. *Damaged in a day raid this historic fortress is wreathed in smoke—once again in the "front line."*

HOME GUARD

IT was on May 14, 1940, that Mr. Anthony Eden broadcast an appeal for Local Defence Volunteers, and the effect was immediately apparent.

Police stations all over Britain were besieged by men anxious to drill and be armed in the face of the invasion that seemed to be inevitable. By October 8, 1940, Mr. Churchill could announce that 1,700,000 men had voluntarily sprung to arms. Brassards bearing the letters "L.D.V." were issued; a multitude of assorted weapons —obsolete rifles, shotguns, a sprinkling of artillery, knives and home-made "coshes"—were handled by men determined to use them to the end if the occasion arose.

It was an eye-opener to Berlin, where Ribbentrop's "Decadent British" theory still held in spite of Dunkirk.

On August 24 Mr. Churchill's new name for the citizen army became adopted, and henceforth it was the "Home Guard." Uniforms were supplied, and from an enthusiastic company of amateurs, the Home Guard became a well-clad, efficiently-equipped, spare-time home army, releasing thousands of serving men for service abroad.

HOME GUARD PROGRESS. *Top left is shown a company of Local Defence Volunteers in the early days ; above, Home Guards seen handling a 3.7 anti-aircraft gun.*

INDUSTRIAL FRONT

IT became apparent to the general public in 1940 that nothing short of total mobilization of the nation's wealth and manpower would defeat and beat the Axis. For the first time the full implications of total war were realized by everybody. Therefore the steps taken by the Government received almost universal support from the men and women of Great Britain.

Clearly Britain's first need was weapons—aircraft, guns, tanks, rifles, mines, bombs and the thousand and one essentials of modern war. To remove obstructive bottlenecks and to prevent waste planning on a scale which would have seemed inconceivable in 1939 had to be rushed through. In practical terms this meant that rigid control of resources, material, and workers had to be exercised.

Lists of priorities were drawn up. When aeroplanes were the most vital need, the aircraft industry had first claim on labour, factory space, and raw materials. Other weapons took a higher or lower place on the lists according to the dictates of the situation.

The workers realized that it was up to them. The trades unions co-operated with the Government in making maximum production possible, whilst safeguarding the welfare and working conditions of the individual. In the factories themselves engineers planned ways of "breaking down" processes to make the maximum use of semi-skilled and unskilled labour, releasing craftsmen for certain essential tasks. Women became crane-drivers, riveters, turners, and tackled many jobs hitherto considered suitable only for men.

TANK TAKES SHAPE. *Long assembly lines in one of Britain's great tank factories mirrors the astonishingly increased tempo.*

" THAT'S ONE OF OURS." *A study in expressions among the London crowds who saw air battles in progress on the outskirts of the capital during the Battle of Britain.*

Time and again the Luftwaffe made all-out daylight attempts to storm through to the heart of the city. Each time outnumbered R.A.F. fighters drove them back with losses.

BATTLE OF BRITAIN

ON the morning of August 8 the "Hamburger Fremdenblatt" announced: "An attack by the mighty forces of Germany will be made on Britain in the near future. Napoleon . . . flinched at the last moment from making the attempt to conquer the island. But under the inspired hand of Adolf Hitler, who is the real Holy Ghost, the modern weapons the Reich possess can, and quickly will, put an end to the insularity of Britain."

On that same morning 400 enemy aircraft launched the first stage of what was to be known as the Battle of Britain. For a month the Luftwaffe had been concentrated on shipping. Now the master-plan was to be put into operation.

Massed formations of bombers (for the most part Ju.87 dive-bombers) were escorted by large fighter formations flying above them. The out-numbered Spitfires and Hurricanes rose to meet the invader. Against the canopy of a summer sky men and women looked up from the south and south-eastern towns to see the fierce dogfights that were to decide, in large part, their destiny.

Thames Estuary attacked

By the evening of the 8th, 21 enemy aircraft were sent crashing into the sea and a total of 60 destroyed.

Three days later the enemy resumed his assault in even greater weight, choosing Portland, Weymouth, and convoys in the Thames Estuary, as targets. Dover's turn came on the 12th and Portsmouth and the Isle of Wight heard the roar and drone of aircraft.

Such a toll had the R.A.F. taken that it became clear to the Germans that the fighter aerodromes of Britain must be destroyed. Therefore, when

FORCED LANDING. *A sergeant pilot jumps the fence of a field in which he has made a forced landing after shooting down his first Messerschmitt over the coast of France.*

READY FOR BATTLE. *In his clumsy flying clothes one of the pilots of a fighter aerodrome is assisted into the cockpit of his machine for an operational sweep.*

1,000 Luftwaffe aircraft swarmed in on the 15th large numbers were detailed to deal with aerodromes in the south and south-east. Some penetrated as far inland as Croydon. They did a certain amount of damage, but at a cost of 180 aircraft destroyed. Dive-bombers shrieked down, not to unload their deadly cargo but to meet a fiery end in English fields; the fighter escorts proved powerless to deal with the dashing attacks of Britons in superior machines.

Air battles were visible from streets and rooftops. Labourers in the fields paused to watch the specks in the sky, and the significant patterns of exhaust smoke.

"I was in a train," said one eye-witness, "when I saw a running fight between a Spitfire and a Messer-schmitt over a stationary train. The Messerschmitt seemed to leap over the train and on its tail was a Spitfire. There was a good deal of twisting and turning for position and in the end the Spitfire brought the Jerry down in flames in a neighbouring field."

Luftwaffe's Losses

By evening on the 15th the Luftwaffe had lost 472 aircraft. Like a gambler heedlessly staking in the face of losses, the enemy flung in between five and six hundred aircraft on August 16 and about the same number two days later. He lost 45 of them. On the 18th one squadron of 13 Hurricanes brought down, without loss, an equal number of the enemy.

Thus in the 10 days' assault the Luftwaffe had lost 697 for certain and the R.A.F. 153, with 60 British pilots safe.

It became apparent to Goering, head of Germany's air force, that radical changes in methods were necessary. He called a halt, and for five days air activity by day, except for reconnaissance, ceased.

On August 20 Mr. Churchill rose from his seat on the Treasury Bench to give a review of the war. In it he spoke the following tribute: "The gratitude of every home in our island, in our Empire, and indeed throughout the world, except in the abodes of the guilty, goes out to the British airmen who, undaunted by odds, unwearied in their constant challenge and mortal danger, are turning the tide of world war by their prowess and by their devotion. Never in the field of human conflict was so much owed by so many to so few."

Dogfights over Dockland

Meanwhile the Germans had been frantically evolving new methods for the resumption of the day offensive in the air. The covering screen of fighters was enlarged and redistributed, and towards the end of this final effort, which lasted until the end of October, the use of heavy bombers was discontinued and fast fighter-bombers substituted. As before, fighter aerodromes were the main target, together with aircraft factories, although civilian targets received many bombs dropped by the Germans as they fled from the avenging British.

On September 7 there was a fight over dockland, followed by incendiaries and high explosive by night. Nevertheless British defences were not caught unprepared by any new tactical device employed. German bombers escaped from our front-line fighters, only to run into the waiting second line. The preparations of the Air Ministry had been comprehensive and complete; our fighters could be switched to the quarter from which danger threatened.

The greatest day in the history of the Royal Air Force was September 15, when the enemy lost 185 planes in one day in battles which raged from Kent to the French coast.

Switch to Night Bombing

As the October days wore on, it became apparent that the Battle of Britain had been won. The Luftwaffe switched their total energy to the terrible, but less effective, task of night-raiding. Many famous buildings had been hit, including Buckingham Palace. In day fights 1,700 people, and by night 12,581, had been killed. But 2,375 German planes had been lost and never again were the R.A.F. to lose the superiority they had established over the Luftwaffe.

In proportion to his great losses, the enemy had achieved remarkably little. He had managed to sink five ships and to damage five more sailing in Channel convoys. Damage had been done to various aerodromes and to the London docks, while production in the factories had been temporarily reduced, though to a negligible extent. But in the military sense the daylight campaign had been one of unmitigated disaster. Hitler's waiting land forces were precisely where they had been when the attack commenced—on the other side of the English Channel.

The time was to come when the other branches of Britain's Fighting Forces were to be in the limelight, but for the time being the deep thankfulness of all free people was to the R.A.F. ; to the British pilots and to their Czech, Polish, French and American colleagues, not forgetting the men who did their duty in the less spectacular but equally vital role of ground staff ; and to the anti-aircraft batteries who themselves accounted for 250 hostile aircraft during the daylight operations.

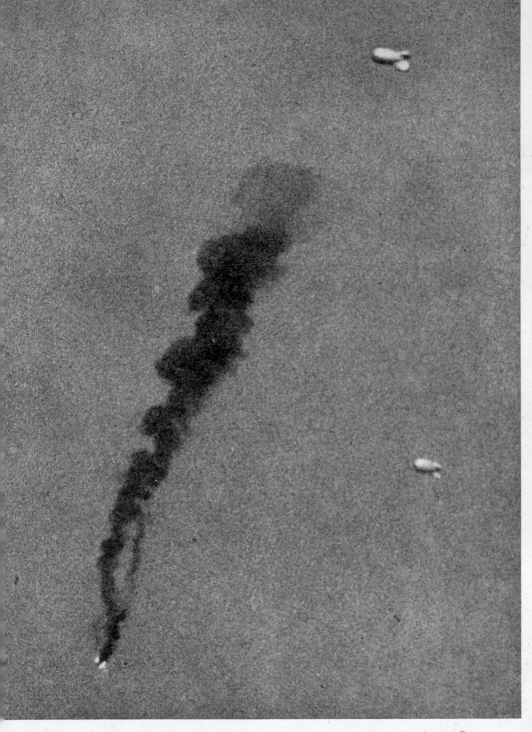

ANOTHER BLOW FOR GOERING. *With black smoke pouring from its fuselage, a German bomber crashes earthwards between the barrage balloons. The scene is near Dover.*

LUFTWAFFE GRAVEYARD. *Wreckage of a crashed German bomber is inspected by R.A.F. technical experts before being taken away to join the growing piles of scrap metal. Some had been brought down by anti-aircraft fire or barrage balloons, the great majority had fallen victim to the skill of the men who piloted Hurricanes and Spitfires.*

Scenes such as this became fairly common throughout Southern England during the summer and autumn of 1940 until the enemy became exhausted by his great air losses. To the trained eye of the examiners each crashed Luftwaffe plane had a story to tell. All changes in design were carefully noted and vital information passed to the R.A.F.

NIGHT IN THE CITY. *Crackle of flames and crash of falling girders form the background to this dramatic scene in Queen Victoria Street. London's firemen, working for hours at a stretch, fight it out with the flames. Such scenes occurred in all directions.*

ATTACK ON LONDON

THE few had won the Battle of Britain, and now the long nights of the second war winter had come. The Luftwaffe, driven from the daylight skies of Britain, now planned to end organized life in the great British towns by sustained attacks under the protection of darkness.

London was the main target. Hitler said that the capital must be "erased." Formerly Londoners had read with incredulous horror of what had happened formerly to Warsaw and Rotterdam. Now it was their turn; they were in the front line, as had been the Poles, Belgians and the Dutch.

Nights of Terror

Night after night the drone of German bombers, circling with apparent leisureliness, and the crash of the all too few anti-aircraft guns, became familiar sounds. The pointing fingers of the searchlight beams, the pin-points of bursting shells against the blackness of the sky, the sinister beauty of flares dropping slowly earthwards, became accustomed sights. The bombers came over in waves, up to 500 machines being employed during one night.

Every morning streets were littered with fragments of broken glass and masonry. A pile of rubble, with perhaps a bath, a pathetic piece of furniture or a torn strip of wall-paper lying apart from the main wreckage, marked what had been a home a few hours previously.

Shops, cinemas and churches, burnt out or destroyed, gaping holes torn in pavements, thoroughfares closed because of delayed action bombs—these things became part and parcel of life in the besieged city and came to be accepted almost without comment.

Men and women streamed home from work in the evenings to snatch a hurried meal before the banshee wail of the sirens announced that the devil's work was about to begin.

Some donned steel helmets and commenced A.R.P. duties. Of the others, some went quietly to bed at the usual time, others made up beds in the "safest" part of the house, or retired to the protection of the Anderson shelters erected in the garden. The public shelters, in basements or underneath stout arches, became warm with the heat of closely packed bodies of shelterers. Some of the shelterers achieved a kind of routine, bringing mattresses, thermos flasks, food for young babies; others snatched a few hours' sleep on a raincoat or blanket. Some congregated in parties; others sat silently alone.

Life in the Shelters

The tube stations were opened at night. At first it was merely a question of finding a space on the platform. Then tiered bunks were provided, canteens and hygiene organized, and while all was inferno in the street impromptu entertainments took place in the safe tunnels beneath the streets.

East and west hundreds of buildings continued to be destroyed. Shelterers emerged into the cold light of the early morning and trudged along scarred streets to see if their homes stood.

Newspaper offices were burned out, famous churches crashed. Piccadilly had a bomb crater in it one morning, with a rushing stream of water from a burst main that gave an odd semblance of rusticity.

The Central Telegraph Office went down, St. Paul's was hit, lovely old

NO MAN'S LAND. *Silhouetted against the flames, London A.R.P. workers scramble across the great piles of tangled wreckage, intent on their job despite falling bombs.*

buildings in the Temple disfigured. The old hall in which Shakespeare's "Twelfth Night" was first produced was destroyed.

Tramways were torn up, viaducts dissolved into ruins, armies of people became homeless.

The House of Commons was damaged and ugly bruises appeared on Westminster Abbey. The Church of St. Clement Danes—Dr. Johnson's church, the children's church with bells that talked of oranges and lemons —became a burnt out shell. Two buses fell into a bomb crater near the Oval and people walked on top of them.

Each morning brought its crop of stories. Two hundred people were trapped and suffocated in a stricken shelter. Postmen could be seen striving to rescue charred letters from torn and twisted boxes, engineers mending smashed underground cables so that communication might be kept open and the daily round in motion.

Huge stores in Oxford Street were gutted, stately homes in Mayfair and squalid tenements in back streets of the East End fell to the ground between sunset and sunrise.

All through the onslaught London's thousands of night workers carried on. The clanging of tram bells and the tooting of taxis were never stilled. The

Through the smoke glimpsed burning buildings as the fire spreads. Wounded have to be tended, trapped shelterers released, fires controlled, communications kept open.

vital night continuity of the vast Post Office organization was not broken. The mails went off with bombs falling about them. Sorters carried on with their work with parts of the building blown away. Telephone switch-board girls stuck to their posts amid flames and smoke caused by incendiaries. The vanmen, postmen and clerks took a quiet pride in sticking it out. The laconic official records tell that between September, 1940, and September, 1941, 3,000 joists, 1,700 cables, and some 500,000 wires were repaired.

The transport workers rallied magnificently to the occasion. Bus drivers and conductors kept the essential communications open. The railway workers occupied a key position and did not falter. Gaping holes in the permanent way were repaired by squads working night and day. Incendiaries falling upon goods vans were quenched at the risk of life and limb. Despite the blitz the goods went through.

The extent of London's ordeal may be gauged from the fact that, from September, 1940, to May, 1941, 1,150,000 houses in the London area were damaged. Billeted as homeless were 375,000 people. More than 30,000 were killed, and 50,000 injured. Thirteen thousand of the killed were women and children.

RESCUE WORK

WHEN a building dissolved into a tangled mass of brickwork and girders, when rows of suburban villas flattened out before the blast from explosives, when shelters became buried under masses of debris, then it was that the tasks of the rescue squads commenced. It was not easy to ascertain whether or not wounded lay pinned under the wreckage and no chances could be taken.

It was hard, dangerous work. Not only did other bombs frequently drop near squads engaged in rescuing the casualties caused by a previous one, but the risk of becoming trapped or injured by crashing walls, falling masonry and girders had constantly to be undertaken.

Hundredweights and even tons of debris had to be removed, tunnels dug through wreckage, girders and iron-work cut through by blow-lamp, before the casualties could be dragged out. Sometimes the task would be a matter of a few hours; in other cases it would be a day, or even days, before the last casualty could be extricated.

Sometimes when the victims were conscious they would hear the blessed sound of deliverance approaching and would call or bang on the ground as an indication of the direction in which they lay. Sometimes pipes would be passed down through a small aperture and food and drink conveyed to those who waited patiently for their release. Doctors would worm their way through narrow spaces into the heart of the wreckage to give morphia or other medical attention to the entombed who lay waiting for rescue.

WHEN DAYLIGHT CAME. *Each morning brought new "incidents." Demolition workers are seen digging for the injured.*

HOSPITALS CARRY ON

On the outbreak of war an Emergency Medical Service was formed which provided machinery for the authorities in vulnerable areas to transfer patients to country districts, where the hospitals had a fixed proportion of beds reserved for air raid casualties, and for the re-distribution of medical, surgical and nursing personnel throughout the country. In addition the areas likely to be attacked assembled sufficient ambulances, stretcher bearers, attendants and drivers to cope with the aftermath of air attack. Hospitals, clinics, dressing centres in the cities were prepared to treat minor injuries and to expedite the attention necessary for the more serious casualties.

It was not possible to evacuate the hospitals to safe areas. The sick have to be tended, babies to be delivered, industrial and road accidents to be provided for, even in the middle of a world war. So the staffs of the hospitals continued their tasks through the months of blitz, the stream of casualties adding to their normal work. One London hospital, St. Thomas's, near Lambeth Bridge, alone received 11 direct hits, many patients and members of the staff being killed or injured.

AMBULANCE AND HOSPITAL. *An L.C.C. ambulance waiting outside a wrecked London building is seen in the photograph on the left. A bus, wrecked by the blast, is a reminder of how communications were kept going through the blitz. Below is shown another London scene—nurses searching the debris at the London Chest Hospital, Victoria Park. The patients and staff had all miraculously survived a direct hit.*

BRITISH ENTER LIBYA. *It is December 16, 1940, and the Italian colony of Libya is entered by the victorious British troops under General Sir Archibald Wavell. An advance armoured force rumbles past the ruins of Fort Capuzzo, south of Bardia. The sudden counterstroke has sent the Italian armies reeling back across the desert.*

FIRST DESERT VICTORY

THE most hopeful news during the summer of 1940 was that the Axis strategy had turned towards the East. The neutrals talked of the master-plan being a drive through Persia, the conquest of India and a link-up between the German-Italian forces with those of Japan.

In Cairo Sir Archibald Wavell had his headquarters, with 30,000 men at his disposal, a seemingly frail barrier against the Axis scheme. Marshal Graziani, Italian Commander in Libya, had 300,000 men ready for action. He advanced through the desert, taking Sollum and Sidi Barrani, but for some reason he did not take the bold action warranted by his superiority in men and materials.

Wavell turns the Tables

Then, by one of the most dramatic strokes in modern warfare, Wavell turned the tables. When his Intelligence learned of a gap in the Italian defensive system to the south-west, the British flooded through it in an attempt to get round the Italian forces. They were successful. By December 12, 1940, Graziani's armies were reeling back, and 20,000 Italians taken prisoner.

At the end of a week's fighting Sollum, Halfaya Pass, Fort Capuzzo, and Sidi Omar had fallen to Wavell's men, and before Christmas 30,000 Italian troops, including five generals, were streaming back to the prison camps. By February 8, 1941, British and Empire forces had pushed on over 500 miles, taking Benghazi, Cyrenaica and all its forts, and were standing far west of Ageila.

The capture of Tobruk may be singled out from the many battles fought by the "desert rats," who sweltered under the parching sun as they thrust their way over the desert. The final assault on the strongly-defended port was launched at dawn on January 21. This was backed by naval and air forces, and as the infantry went forward behind their cover of artillery and tanks the defenders showed by their spirited resistance the importance of the town to the Italians. Australian troops, who led the attack, again distinguished themselves by their great dash.

Britain keeps Faith

"On to Tripoli" was the call now. But faced with the imminent collapse of his Italian satellites, Hitler sent his best troops into action. On April 6, without warning, Germany invaded Yugoslavia and Greece. From both came a call Britain could not refuse.

There was a synchronized landing of German mechanized units on the west coast of Cyrenaica, and before the new threat General Sir Henry Maitland Wilson moved back. The British Government, called upon to make an historic decision, transferred supporting troops from Egypt to help Greece.

The Mediterranean War had embarked upon a new stage. The smashing of the Italian North African armies had been accomplished with small losses.

On the other hand the Germans still possessed superiority on land, and the Nazi panzers rolled along the coastal road in Cyrenaica, entering Benghazi on April 3. Although the British were forced to abandon most of the territory they had won, they continued to hold on to Tobruk. Supplied by food and munitions by sea, the heroic garrison were to hold on until the next phase of the battle for Africa.

WAR IN THE BALKANS

EARLY in October, 1940, the Italian press campaign against Greece, which had begun by accusing her of fomenting disorder in Albania and rapidly degenerated into demands for territory, reached its peak. Doubtless Mussolini thought that a small and poor country offered an easy victory to offset the military triumphs of Germany, and Hitler agreed to leave this stage in the programme of world domination to the Italians.

On October 28, the Greek Prime Minister, General Metaxas, rejected an Italian ultimatum. Half an hour before its expiration Italian forces, operating from Albania, attacked Greek territory. Winston Churchill sent the following message to the Greeks: "We will give you all the help in our power. We fight a common foe and will share a united victory."

Mussolini had concentrated 100,000 troops on the Greek frontier. For a time they exploited their initial advantage, but then, among the moun-

BATTLE OF THE SNOWS. *Erecting their tents amid the ice and snow of the Albanian Highlands, these tough Greek soldiers prepare to bivouac for the night. Outnumbered by the better-clad Italians, they consistently out-manœuvred and out-generalled them.*

MULE COLUMN. *Tanks and armoured transport were little use in the Albanian cam-paign. Greek evzones with sure-footed mules covered many miles a day with full equip-ment. This picture was taken at a time when Mussolini was visiting the Italian front.*

tains and snows, the Greeks delighted friendly onlookers and astonished the Italians by winning victory after victory. Their counter-attack in Eastern Albania pushed the Italians relentlessly back towards Koritza, Albania's largest town, and on November 22 they captured it with many prisoners and guns. The fall of Pogradets and Premeti was not long delayed. The battles were essentially those of physical toughness and endurance, supplies being taken along mountain roads by mules, and the men bivouacking for the night among the snows. The *evzones*, as the Greek soldiers became known to the western world, were hardier and far better able to hold their own in these

conditions than their Italian counter-parts, whilst the modern weapons possessed by the enemy could not be used to full effect in the type of mountain fighting that ensued.

Germany Strikes Again

The Royal Air Force and the small but brave Greek Air Force helped to confuse and impede the retreating Italians; convoys of supplies of all kinds were sent from Britain.

Then, on the morning of April 6, the world learned that German armies had attacked Greece and Yugoslavia. The British reply was given promptly. More men and materials were sent to aid the Greeks without delay; and they had to be furnished from the Middle East, where they were also needed. Armies, many of them made up of Australians and New Zealanders, were transported to Greece and soon Anzac boys, descendants of those who gave immortality to their kind at Gallipoli, were about the classic ways of Athens.

Proud of their new mission, Lieut.-General Sir Thomas Blamey, the Australian Commander-in-Chief, gave this address to his men when they touched Greek soil:

"Just 26 years ago the Australian Army carried out the first operation on the Northern Mediterranean shores when our kinsmen landed at Gallipoli. We have now landed again in these regions to fight at the side of the Greeks and overthrow once more the German effort to enslave the world. The Greek nation, the smallest and poorest of all the nations the Axis has sought to bully into submission, refused to submit. Their efforts, along with our own, have already destroyed one of the Axis partners as a Power and forced Germany to take control of Italy's destiny. There can be no doubt also that their valiant and successful struggle had a great effect in determining Yugoslavia, after she had yielded to German bullying, to arise and defy the Axis powers."

Heroic Rearguard

Greeks, Englishmen, Yugoslavs, Australians, New Zealanders, they all put up a grand fight—but it was obvious early that the organized, numerically overwhelming, and perfectly equipped German forces, working easily from land communications and interior lines, added up to a tide that could not be stemmed. There was desperate defensive fighting by the Allies about Athens and on the old battlefields of Thermopylæ. Again the German barbarians swarmed about the Acropolis and the nursery of civilized enlightenment was once more trampled underfoot by the invading Hun.

Yugoslavian Drama

Concluding stages of the Greek drama were paralleled by the equally significant happenings in Yugoslavia.

Firstly, the pro-German Government of the Regent, Prince Paul, had been swept away in a wave of popular indignation during March, and an all-party Government under General Simovitch formed. Then began the chorus of Nazi threats, culminating in invasion on April 6.

Subsequent events—the organization of partisan warfare on an unequalled scale—proved the boundless courage of the Yugoslavs. But they were powerless to resist the German machine in terms of formal war. This was proved by savage bombing attacks upon Belgrade in the morning of April 6, in spite of it having been declared an open city. Suffice it to say that the toll of destruction rivalled the horrors of Warsaw and Rotterdam.

On April 12, Belgrade was occupied. In lively anticipation of the kill the Hungarians, who had signed a pact of " eternal friendship " with Yugoslavia the previous February, seized large areas of territory. Broken and battered, the Yugoslav forces were split into groups. As will be seen from the map on the opposite page, German strategy was to drive forward to Belgrade, while the southern pincer struck down towards the Greeks fighting in Albania.

On April 17, the Germans could announce that organized resistance was at an end. The kill had been made, but Yugoslavia was to have her revenge, and to become one of the first liberated Allied countries.

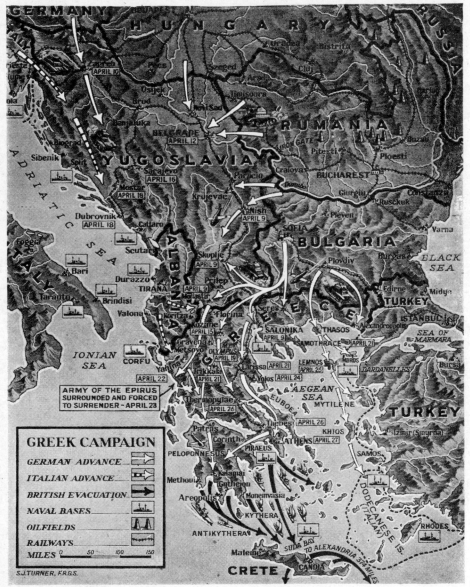

GERMANY HUNGARY RUMANIA RUSSIA
Zagreb APRIL 10
Bihac
Banjaluka
Biograd
Sibenik
Split
YUGOSLAVIA
Sarajevo APRIL 16
Mostar APRIL 18
Dubrovnik APRIL 18
Cattaro
Scutari
ADRIATIC SEA
Bari
Durazzo
TIRANA
Taranto
Brindisi
Valona
ALBANIA
IONIAN SEA
CORFU
APRIL 22
Bistrita
Cluj
Belgrade APRIL 12
IRON GATE
Pitesti
Ploesti
BUCHAREST
Giurgiu
Ruscuk
Constanza
Krujevac
Nish APRIL 9
SOFIA
BULGARIA
Skupile APRIL 9
Prilep
Florina
SALONIKA APRIL 9
SAMOTHRACE
LEMNOS APRIL 23
GREECE
OLYMPIA
Larissa APRIL 21
Yolos APRIL 24
Plovdiv
Burgas
BLACK SEA
Edirne
Midye
TURKEY
ISTANBUL
SEA OF MARMARA
Bursa
DARDANELLES

ARMY OF THE EPIRUS
SURROUNDED AND FORCED
TO SURRENDER - APRIL 23

Thermopylae APRIL 26
Patras
Corinth
Methoni
Areopoli
ANTIKYTHERA
Maleme
Thebes APRIL 26
PIRAEUS
PELOPONNESUS
Kalamai
Gytheion
Monemvasia
KYTHERA
AEGEAN SEA
MYTILENE
ATHENS APRIL 27
KHIOS
SAMOS
SUDA BAY
CANDIA
CRETE
TURKEY
Izmir (Smyrna)
DODECANESE (ITALIAN)
RHODES
TO ALEXANDRIA 374 MILES

GREEK CAMPAIGN

GERMAN ADVANCE	
ITALIAN ADVANCE	
BRITISH EVACUATION	
NAVAL BASES	
OILFIELDS	
RAILWAYS	
MILES	0 50 100 150

S.J.TURNER, F.R.G.S.

GERMAN BALKAN DRIVE. *The map above illustrates the stages of the enemy's campaign which culminated in the evacuation of Greece by the Allies and paved the way to the successful air attack on the Greek island of Crete. This not only gave Germany many strategically valuable sea and air bases, but also guarded the mineral and agricultural wealth of the Balkans, upon which the Axis had increasingly to rely. It brought the German sphere of influence to the border of the Black Sea, and this was an important factor in view of Hitler's plan to attack Russia, which he put into execution two months after the Allied withdrawal from Greece, which was completed by May 3, 1941.*

BATTLE OF THE ATLANTIC

BRITISH and Allied sailors and ships were the foundation upon which all British strategy had in the final analysis to be based.

When the Germans sunk the defenceless *Athenia*, with 1,400 Anglo-American civilian passengers aboard, on September 4, 1939, they showed they meant to attack Britain's sea lines even more ruthlessly than in the First World War. From the beginning it was apparent that the outcome of the war very largely depended upon Britain and America keeping control of the great Atlantic sea lane, and so in 1940 and 1941 the Battle of the Atlantic became one which had to be fought to a decision. If Britain lost it meant that victories obtained elsewhere would become useless.

" Destroyers, more Destroyers ! "

When Italy joined Germany 118 Italian submarines were added to Hitler's swarms of U-boats. Almost all the French convoy-escorting ships were withdrawn from support, and the European coastline was available to the Germans for bases from which to launch their assault. In the July of 1940 313,000 tons of Allied shipping were sunk in the Atlantic. Long-range German bombers went out to support the attacking U-boats. As Nelson once sent the appeal: "Frigates, more frigates," so British sailors now sent up the cry, "Destroyers, more destroyers." For in spite of our vast Navy insufficient escorting vessels existed to carry out the tasks which arose each month. Lurking U-boats were quick to exploit the opportunities which presented themselves when a convoy was sparsely guarded.

Then a magnificent gesture from the American people was announced by President Roosevelt. Fifty over-age destroyers were to be exchanged with Britain for certain strategic bases which were to be leased to the United States. Protests from the Axis were inevitable and received short shrift. "No combination of dictator countries can stop the help we shall give to the last of the free people," replied Roosevelt, by this time elected for his third term as President of the United States. In his broadcast answer, Winston Churchill responded: "Thrice-chosen head of a hundred and thirty million people, here is the answer I give—put your confidence in us, give us your faith and your blessing, and under Providence all will be well. We shall not fail or falter, we shall not weaken nor tire—give us the tools and we will finish the job."

September and November, 1940, were, nevertheless, black months at sea. Each day the German Press and radio put out alarming stories of the tonnage sunk by their sea raiders. Their claims were much exaggerated and even absurd, but the real facts were grave enough—303,627 tons of British shipping had been sent to the bottom in November alone. This was a trifle better than the August figures which reached the aggregate of 500,000 tons, but the situation was still very grave.

Hitler's Confidence

This meant that ships were being destroyed faster than they could be built or repaired. For a long time the issue swayed in the balance. Hitler opened 1941 with a confident message that the Atlantic was to be closed to Britain. "We have been waiting for our new U-boats," he continued. "In March and April a naval warfare will

THEY SURVIVED. *After drifting for days on a raft, short of food and water, these exhausted survivors from a torpedoed British ship are hauled aboard by friendly hands.*

H. L. W.—D*

WHO GOES THERE ? *One of the many specially-equipped long-distance aircraft of Coastal Command sights a wallowing, heavy-laden tanker. Is it an enemy or a friend?*

start such as the enemy has never expected. Wherever British ships cruise our U-boats will be sent against them until the hour for decision arrives." And the month of May brought the rising curve of German successes to its highest peak. And in spite of their immense casualties the men of the Merchant Navy held steady. Tramps still plodded, hull down, back and forward across the Atlantic, oil tankers and merchant vessels carrying countless varieties of food and munitions, machinery and raw materials braved the sudden encounter with the underwater sniper that cost scores of good ships and thousands of brave men. *Arandora Star, Rawalpindi, Empress of Britain, Dunbar Castle, Rangitane, Jervis Bay, Laurentic, Simon Bolivar*—these are but a few of names that have an honoured place in the list.

After signals have been answered satisfactorily by the tanker, it is allowed to go on its way. These essential air operations were undertaken daily, in good weather or bad.

Gradually, however, what Mr. Churchill called the "apparatus of sea control" began to work. Long range Catalina aircraft of Coastal Command, fast armed escort vessels, improved apparatus for detecting the U-boat, and the increased tempo of shipbuilding all contributed towards bringing the danger under control, but the process was slow, and only made possible by the bravery of the Merchant Navy.

In fact the Battle of the Atlantic, although lulls occurred while the U-boats were refitted, was the longest battle of the war. Improvements in technique by the hunters were met by fresh devices invented by the hunted. Only unceasing vigilance and devotion to duty made the invasion of Germany possible in the face of determined efforts by the enemy to sink supplies being sent by sea to Britain.

IN NORTHERN WATERS. *For long months units of the Royal Navy remained at sea, monotonous convoy duty being relieved by sudden calls to action against U-boats.*

This photograph shows men of H.M.S. Scylla thawing out anchor chains and winches, all frozen hard by a bitter spell of weather far out in the North Atlantic.

ANOTHER CHURCH GUTTED.   *St. Clement Danes, the historic church at the junction of the Strand and Fleet Street, London, was gutted during the night of April 10–11, 1941.*

LONDON IN FLAMES

MAY 10, 1941, marked one of the greatest attempts by the enemy to render London uninhabitable, to paralyse this great city from the air. And the weapon chosen to do this was fire.

The Luftwaffe dumped thousands upon thousands of incendiary bombs upon the capital—every one of them a potential source of danger. To ensure that the fires should spread, high explosives were dropped in sufficient quantities to break water mains, rendering the pumps and hose-pipes useless.

Work of the A.F.S.

The men, and women, who fought and won this great battle were those attached to the London Fire Brigades, professionals, who knew every trick of fire-fighting, and men and women of the Auxiliary Fire Service. Personnel of the latter had in most cases never seen a fire before the raids on London began.

The greatest problem on that memorable night was the number of calls received. The women who "manned" the control rooms frequently found new, urgent demands for assistance piling up when all pumps and personnel were engaged elsewhere. Lightning decisions had to be made, the tired, sweating men who came back from one fire in a state of exhaustion were ordered out again into the night. Pumps hurrying to rush calls found the roads blocked by craters and rubble. Risks had to be taken, and it needed nerves of steel to concentrate upon work when bombs were falling all around.

A fire at the Elephant and Castle, south of the river Thames and the heart of one of London's most thickly populated areas, developed into an inferno because the water mains had been cut.

Seventeen men were killed when a chance hit was scored near a big emergency water supply ; worse still, the entrance to the water supply was blocked. Hose lines to the Thames, over a mile away, were hit and the precious water supply dwindled to a mocking trickle before drying up completely. Not until next day was sufficient water obtained, relayed through nine miles of hose, to get this outbreak under control.

Westminster Abbey was at one time threatened ; happily, the emergency water supply was not hit and the flames were quickly extinguished. Other churches were gutted, office buildings reduced to charred shells, while warehouses, with precious stocks of goods and raw materials, reddened the sky with an unearthly glow.

What Londoners Saw

London that night was a sight never to be forgotten. The air was filled with strange sounds, among them the urgent clangour of fire and ambulance bells, the crackle of flames and the crash of masonry. Overhead droned the German aeroplanes, answered by the chorus of anti-aircraft fire. Over the city itself, reflected from the clouds, was a blood-red halo. In the streets the sickly light from many fires threw the scene into a grotesque caricature of normal human activity. For miles outside the vast area directly affected the glow could be seen.

Too great praise cannot be given to firemen themselves, some of whom literally worked until they dropped, their bodies unequal to their spirit. It was due to their almost superhuman endurance that the enemy did not achieve his purpose and, temporarily at any rate, erase London from the slate. Many of them—in common with other

DURING A RAID—AND AFTER. (*Above*) *Thousands of gallons of water brought through hose-pipes laid from the Thames are pumped on a blazing block of business offices during the great raid on May 10–11, 1941. (Right) Old buildings in Paternoster Row, a short distance from St. Paul's Cathedral, are being demolished after the raid.*

A.R.P. workers—received injuries, sometimes trivial but sometimes serious or fatal. When one remembers that the whole system of wartime fire-fighting had been built up in a comparatively short space of time, with few precedents to consult for guidance, the magnitude of this home-front effort becomes apparent. One's realization is helped by the fact that some of the fires were thirty or forty times as large as London's largest peace-time conflagration and that damage to roads and pavements isolated districts from all outside help for hours at a time.

The lessons learned from bitter experience were scientifically applied when, in the August of 1941, the National Fire Service absorbed and reorganized the system of separate local brigades. In addition, the provision of emergency water supplies, strategically situated to prevent a recurrence of any shortage, ended the dangers that the fire-fighters had to contend with in this direction. One further change, made in the September, was the introduction of the term Civil Defence to include the Fire Service as well as the former A.R.P. workers.

COVENTRY

COVENTRY, a city of 250,000 inhabitants, at once a cathedral town and an important manufacturing area, received its blow on November 14, 1940. In the annals of British air raids, among all the sorrowful and ghastly stories that were recorded during the German effort to break the spirit of the civilian population, the story of Coventry stands out. In the space of a few hours 400 enemy aircraft, in one of the first concentrated air attacks of the war, dropped a greater weight of incendiaries and high explosives on the city than any area of its size in Great Britain had known.

To those thousands of people who were aroused by the wail of the sirens the night can never be forgotten. The Cathedral was bombed and all round it the buildings at the centre of the town reeled and collapsed as the bombs shrieked down. Fire broke out, the more terrifying because the hydrants had in many cases been buried by debris. A canal and the river provided an inadequate source of water.

Roads became impassable as the flames spread and buildings crashed down. There was no escape, nor was there panic. Citizens of this Warwickshire town "took it," as Britons had at Dunkirk and in London.

Next day lorries and cars carrying salvage apparatus, food, clothes and comfort for the people were rushed from neighbouring towns. The homeless were cared for, the injured taken to hospital, and the debris cleared. But the word "Coventry" came to mean the same as Rotterdam and Belgrade.

RUINED CATHEDRAL. *Four walls of Coventry Cathedral stand in silent witness to the indiscriminate night terror.*

115

SOUTHAMPTON'S TURN. *Twisted girders, fallen brickwork, a few buildings miraculously left standing—this was Southampton's High Street after repeated heavy German bombing. Thousands of people were rendered homeless. Hundreds were killed.*

As demolition proceeds, and water, gas and electricity supplies are hurriedly impro-vised, A.R.P. workers, troops and civilians somehow manage to raise a cheerful smile as they trudge along what had once been a very prosperous shopping centre.

117

MYSTERY OF RUDOLPH HESS

"RUDOLPH HESS, deputy Fuehrer of Germany, and Party Leader of the National-Socialist Party, has landed in Scotland." So began a statement issued from 10, Downing Street, on May 12, 1941.

Facts were these. On the night of May 10 a Messerschmitt 110 was reported to be flying in the direction of Glasgow. Since this plane would not have the fuel to return to Germany the report was at first disbelieved. Later, however, the machine crashed near Glasgow, with its guns unloaded.

A luxuriously dressed German officer was found with his ankle broken and was taken to a Glasgow hospital. He said his name was Horn, but subsequently claimed to be Rudolph Hess, and produced photographs to prove it.

From Whitehall an expert was despatched, and the man's identity proved beyond doubt. Medical opinion was called in, and Hess's health and sanity established. He was then removed to confinement as a prisoner of war.

Meanwhile the Nazi radio had broadcast the story that Hess had set off from Augsburg in a plane and had not returned. It was claimed that he was suffering at the time from a mental disorder.

The democracies seethed with rumours. Various speculations were made, particularly when it was officially announced that Hess had tried to obtain interviews with various public figures whom he quite wrongly assumed "Anti-Churchill."

It was not for some time that it became possible to decide what were the real motives behind the affair. It became accepted that Hess, with or without the consent of his rivals in the Nazi party, had attempted to induce Britain to "bury the hatchet with Germany, to forget the horrors of Warsaw, Rotterdam and Coventry, and to join with Hitler against Russia.

PERFECT ARYAN. *Dark, thin-lipped, handsome Rudolph Hess, Hitler's deputy, was boosted by the controlled German Press as the "model German."*

AIR LESSON OF CRETE

STRANGE and savage was the struggle for Crete in May, 1941. British and Empire troops had abundant ships, but no reinforcements, few guns, and no aircraft. The Germans had a mechanized army, but no means of getting it to Crete except by air. As the island is 150 miles from Greece, and Admiral Cunningham's forces held the sea, the defence seemed to have a good chance, but the enemy's air power made the Navy's task too costly, and Crete fell.

Withdrawal of the R.A.F.

There had been a lull of three weeks since the evacuation of Greece. On Crete the Allies massed 28,000 men—British, Australians and New Zealanders, and some Greeks. Their commander, General Freyberg, V.C., lacked proper staff, had no artillery worth mentioning and too few A.A. guns. Since the enemy possessed ample air resources on the mainland, it was decided to withdraw the R.A.F. from the island's small airfields—Maleme, Retimo and Herakleion.

There were few roads in Crete, which added to the British difficulties. No sooner had the air umbrella retired than the enemy's appeared. They bombed the three airports, and on May 20 were dropping parachute troops—crack units of the German army—by the thousand.

Gliders in constant procession were towed by Ju.22 aircraft. The slow-moving air convoys offered a good target; many were shot down and the passengers burned to death, but sufficient got through to start an attack. Cycles, machine guns, food and ammunition were landed. The two other airfields—and, worse still, Suda Bay, the only anchorage to the north—were attacked simultaneously.

The Allies took a fearful toll of their assailants, the Australians particularly distinguishing themselves, hurling them out of Retimo and completely mastering them at Herakleion. But the capture of Maleme enabled the enemy to operate his air shuttle service, pouring in reinforcements every few minutes. On the night of May 21 the Germans essayed a crossing by sea, using transports, light coastal boats captured in Greece, and with an escort of Italian E-boats and destroyers.

They ran right into the British Fleet, which picked them out by searchlights and mercilessly shelled them.

Abandoning the attempt the enemy concentrated his full fury from the air upon the British warships. The cruisers *Gloucester* and *Fiji* were sunk, as well as the fine destroyers *Juno*, *Kelly*, *Kashmir* and *Greyhound*, with the loss of half their crews. Among survivors from *Kelly* was her captain, Lord Louis Mountbatten.

Heroic Rearguard

Meanwhile the island itself was littered with the wreckage of German planes and equipment, with the invaders still pouring in and gradually assuming the dominant role.

On May 27 it was decided to abandon the struggle. Two thousand marines formed a heroic rearguard near the scene of the main fighting; behind this the larger part of the Allied troops crossed the mountainous core of the island to Sphakia, where they were taken off. There was no surrender, few except wounded men falling into the enemy's hands. But dive bombing had now become incessant and only about half got away.

DEADLY "MUSHROOMS." *While one of their great transport planes screams earthward in flames, the German paratroopers float slowly down on to the island of Crete.*

Many of these crack air-borne troops were killed before they reached land, but they were too strong in numbers to be long repelled by the Allied garrison, who lacked air cover.

BISMARCK MEETS HER END

IT was vital to Germany to strangle Britain's sea-borne traffic; it was equally vital to Britain to prevent her. The great battle cruisers *Scharnhorst* and *Gneisenau*, after causing much destruction in the western Atlantic, had run for safety to Brest, where they were systematically bombed during April and May, 1941. Then came the alarming news that on May 21 *Bismarck* had put to sea. The Navy leaped for joy, but the commander-in-chief, Admiral Sir John Tovey, carried a terrible responsibility, for *Bismarck* was strong enough and fast enough, if she once got away, to fight off any but capital ships, while by means of her own aircraft she could sink any merchantmen afloat without even her maintop appearing over the horizon. It was at once decided that the German warship *must* not escape.

At evening on May 23, she was picked up steaming for Iceland in snowy, squally weather. The cruisers *Norfolk* and *Suffolk* trailed her and a trap laid to catch her in Denmark Strait, between Iceland and Greenland. Under forced draught the newest battleship in the Fleet, H.M.S. *Prince of Wales*, together with the giant battle cruiser *Hood*, found their quarry.

LAST MOMENTS OF H.M.S. "HOOD." *Hit in the magazine by a chance shell from the hunted* Bismarck, *H.M.S.* Hood *is enveloped by the smoke from a huge explosion before she rapidly sinks. All her crew of 1,500, except three, went down with their ship.*

"BISMARCK" SURVIVORS. *Saved from drowning by the British, these crestfallen young Bismarck sailors refuse to look at the camera on their arrival at London. For the duration their "living space" will be behind the wire of an internment camp.*

They opened fire and scored hits, but the enemy's shooting was more successful. *Prince of Wales* was hit and lost contact. *Hood*, show ship of the Royal Navy, received a blow in the magazine, went up in an awful explosion, and all her crew of 1,500, except three, perished with her. The enemy, on fire, disappeared, and was lost for 31 hours.

Dramatic Knock-out

Admiral Tovey now took a bold decision. He felt certain that *Bismarck* would make for a French port, and he ordered his ships accordingly. A squadron came up from Gibraltar. *Rodney* and the flagship, H.M.S. *King George V*, were west of Iceland. Aircraft systematically combed the sea from above in a careful pattern; and at last the quarry was sighted about 500 miles west of Brest. At once the hornets of *Ark Royal* went into action.

The sea was rough and they had great difficulty in landing and taking off, but although there were some crashes and several false flights, at last they found *Bismarck* and torpedoed her. She was struck astern and badly damaged, her speed falling to eight knots; then a second torpedo hit her amidships and she began to wander round in circles. It was now Monday night, wild and grey.

Admiral Luetjens, the enemy commander, telegraphed home: "Ship unmanœuvrable, but will fight to the last shell." This was no mere boast. During the night the destroyers *Cossack* and *Maori* closed with the stricken giant, planting two more torpedoes.

With dawn aircraft went over again; and shortly before 9 a.m. *Rodney* and *King George V* came into action, reducing *Bismarck* to a mere floating wreck. Then, at 11 a.m., *Dorsetshire* was sent in to torpedo her once more and, flag still flying, she sank. Whatever her mission may have been, it ended at the bottom of the Atlantic.

CHIVALRY AT SEA. *Not long before they had been enemies; now they are men struggling in the sea. A British warship bears down to pick up members of* Bismarck's *crew.*

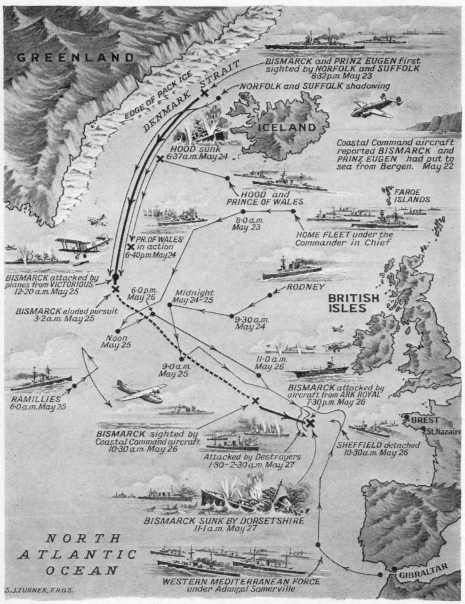

PURSUIT OF "BISMARCK." *Shown pictorially in the above map, the stages in the 1,700-mile chase which resulted in the sinking of Bismarck may be clearly followed. First sighted off Greenland on the evening of May 23, she endeavoured for nearly four days to shake off her pursuers. After sinking Hood and running the gauntlet until the early morning of May 25, she disappeared. A brilliant piece of deduction by Admiral Tovey enabled a squadron coming from Gibraltar to relocate her, and in the morning of May 27, 1941, she was finally sent to the bottom by the torpedoes of the Dorsetshire.*

PART THREE

WORLD
IN FLAMES

RUSSIAN GLORY

FOR more than a year the Russians had remained deeply concerned spectators of the war. For a time it looked as though all western Europe outside their frontiers would disappear underneath the Nazi flood and that Russia would have finally to face a triumphant and irresistible enemy, thirsting to achieve Hitler's well-known ambition of securing the Ukraine and Caucasus as *lebensraum* for his master race and as a doorway to his Empire of the East.

As the British nation firmly withstood the heaviest blows that the Germans could administer, as her young men took to the sky and defeated the cream of the Luftwaffe, as her armies and Navy remained ready to defend her islands to the last, the Russians shrewdly utilized their time. Their air force was doubled; shadow factories sprang up safe behind the Ural Mountains; German military strategy was carefully studied.

Early in the June of 1941 rumours began to circulate that Hitler was pressing demands on Russia for territorial and other concessions, backing his arguments by massed troops. Some people began to speculate whether Russia would attempt appeasement. Those who knew her said: "She will certainly resist." The course of events proved Russia's will to resist.

RUSSIA'S AGONY. *Russian peasants ensure that no grain remains for the Germans in this huge, burned-out granary.*

127

GERMAN ADVANCE GUARD. *As they rake a small Russian town with machine-gun fire before the order is given to occupy it, forward German units see it scorched.*

EASTERN FRONT

A T 4 a.m. on June 22, 1941, German troops poured across the frontier without warning. German aircraft attacked Sebastopol, Kiev and other cities. Later in the day the German Ambassador presented Molotov with a lengthy farrago of complaints.

Now began the most colossal struggle the world had witnessed. The war of 1914-18 had seen armies totalling several millions opposing each other over several battle zones. Against Russia Hitler was able to send over four million front-line troops with an equal number in reserve. As usual the Germans relied upon the paralysing punching power of their armoured divisions, backed by the Luftwaffe, artillery, and highly mobile infantry.

Race against Winter

Speed was the keynote of the German attack, with Moscow as the objective which had to be reached before winter. Four big thrusts were launched: through the Baltic States to capture Leningrad; a second through central Poland to drive on Moscow; a third through southern Poland at the northern Ukraine; while a fourth, from Roumania, was to strike along the north shore of the Black Sea, taking Odessa and the Crimea on its way to the oil fields of the Caucasus.

At the outset the German masses advanced like an irresistible tide. Stalin was too wise to risk letting his main forces be shattered by the first smashing impact of German armour, and it was not until the third day that the invaders made contact with Russian regular troops. Then they found themselves checked in a succession of grim delaying actions. It took them a vital month to establish themselves across the frontiers of Russia proper. But an army in retreat cannot avoid losses, and the Russian armies, swinging slowly back to avoid encirclement, suffered grievously in men and material.

Britain's Support

From Britain, Winston Churchill made his country's attitude clear beyond doubt when he declared in a broadcast: "We shall give whatever help we can to Russia and the Russian people. We shall appeal to all our friends and allies in every part of the world to take the same course and pursue it, as we shall, faithfully and steadfastly to the end!"

The impetus of the German thrusts for a time centred north and south: up towards Leningrad, south towards the Ukraine. By the end of August the enemy had overrun all Estonia, capturing and burning Tallinn, and were nearing Leningrad, Russia's traditional "window to the West." The western Ukraine was in German hands; their troops had forced a crossing of the River Dneiper and taken the great industrial centre of Dneipropetrovsk. The battles were all on a gigantic scale, huge masses of men and steel being hurled together as the Germans clawed tigerishly at the defences and the Russians, torn and bleeding, struck back at their assailants.

As the great struggle progressed, it became apparent that Hitler's main drive was upon Moscow. He fancied that by capturing the heart of Russia he would be master of the whole. But his first rush was checked, slowed down, and bogged by a series of engagements in the area of Smolensk. After six weeks of bitter struggle he was still held there, half-way to his goal.

GERMAN FRIGHTFULNESS

IN the vast areas that fell for a time into German hands, cruelty and, at best, indifference towards the native population prevailed. In German eyes the Slavs were a sub-race whose extermination, apart from those to be used as slaves, was a matter of policy. There were, too, many Jews who, in Nazi estimation, were only fit for annihilation. A period of horror ensued.

Later a Soviet State Commission was set up to sift the facts. This is some of those they found. At Orel more than 30,000 citizens and prisoners of war were butchered. At Smolensk the total reached 135,000. Two small but fully documented instances are typical. At Sychevka, on December 10, 1942, 34 Russians were forced to dig their own graves and were then shot. In the same district on January 7, 1943, 100 Jewish women, old people and children, were driven on to a mined road and blown up. Others were tortured in sport by the Nazis.

The Russians tried four war criminals when they re-entered Kharkov. One of the accused, a German officer, named Langheld, had six women flogged, all of whom died. One had a child, who clung to her and cried. Asked what became of the child, Langheld replied: "The lance corporal who was to take away the woman's body got tired of it and shot the child. Such things happen everywhere. It is our system."

VILLAGERS AND VILLAGE HOMES. (*Left*) *Two women, driven bare-footed from their small cottage by German soldiers, stand and weep at what they see. (Below) An evacuated village in the Russian Ukraine is wreathed in smoke and flames. It has been fired by the inhabitants as a duty to their country before the enemy arrives.*

SACRIFICE FOR FREEDOM

Among, the hard decisions forced upon the Soviet Government the order to destroy the great Dnieper Dam, near Zaporohze, stands out. The dam itself stood for so much, quite apart from the fact that it was among the world's largest. It had been erected under the First Five-Year-Plan, with a double object; first to flood the rapids which for 55 miles obstruct the middle Dnieper between its two navigable bends. Second, and still more important, to create a head of water from which hydro-electric power could be supplied.

The power thus obtained had enabled thriving industries to develop in what had been nothing but corn and mining country. It formed the first step in a power scheme which spread to the more valuable Don Basin beyond. Life and light, machines and traction, where for ages the peasant's cart had rolled and industrialization been unknown, sprang from the almost limitless power that was generated.

A huge power station had been built; this, too, had to be put out of the enemy's reach. The dam itself was a massive concrete wall more than 120 feet high and 800 yards long across the river. The rise of water level reached 110 feet, submerging the rapids and spreading far beyond the Dnieper's former banks. Huge flumes trapped the water, transforming it into energy.

In August, 1941, holes were drilled and explosives laid. On the 25th von Kleist and his Germans reached Dniepropetrovsk, and two days later the order went forth: "Blow up the dam." The pressure of a button, a mighty roar, a cloud of dust, the rush of water through the gap, and it was all over.

SACRIFICE FOR FREEDOM. *(Left), a miracle of modern engineering, the Dnieper Dam which provided electric current for Russia's largest industrial region. (Below), the harnessed water is freed as the Russians blow an enormous breach in the dam walls.*

RUSSIA'S GREAT LEADER. *Joseph Vissarionovich Stalin, Russia's greatest states-man, initiated the scorched earth campaign and guerilla warfare against the aggressor.*

STALIN GIVES HIS PLAN

OF all the world's statesmen Joseph Vissarionovich Stalin, who was in his sixty-second year when the Germans marched into Russia, had been the most inscrutable to western eyes. His official pronouncements and press interviews had been few and generally terse; his power came not from the leadership of a Parliament but from his position as general secretary of the Russian Communist Party. Nevertheless he had seen the course of Hitlerite Germany towards a bid for world domination from the beginning. For instance, he solemnly observed to a congress of his party on January 26, 1934, that: "Quite clearly, things are moving towards a new war."

When the new war came Russia was not unprepared. Stalin, who had first proved his organizational ability and grasp of military strategy during the hard fighting on Russian soil which followed the Bolshevik Revolution, led his country through defeats and hardships unparalleled in history.

Gravity of the Situation

The following points were made by Stalin during the course of his broadcast to the Russian people on June 3, in which he outlined the policy of resistance to the German invaders:

"I am addressing myself to you, in the grave moment of the attacks of Hitler's Germany on our Fatherland. In spite of the heroic resistance of the Red Army, in spite of the fact that the best divisions of the enemy and the best units of his air force have already been beaten and have found their graves on the battlefields, the enemy continues to push forward and to throw new forces on the front . . .

Are the German-Fascist armies really invincible, as is continually proclaimed by the boastful Fascist propagandists? History shows that there are no invincible armies . . .

"Our resistance to the enemy increases and grows. The entire Soviet people is rising in defence of the Fatherland at the side of the Red Army. Our enemy is cruel and merciless. He intends to seize our land, bathed in our sweat, to seize our wheat and oil, the fruits of our labour . . . it is therefore a question of life and death for the Soviet State—a question of whether the peoples of the Soviet Union shall be free or whether they shall be reduced to slavery.

Organizing Guerilla Warfare

"In the event of the retreat of the Red Army all railway rolling stock must be brought away. We must not leave a single engine, a single railway coach, a single pound of grain or a single gallon of petrol to the enemy. The collective farmers must take away all their cattle and place their corn in the care of State organizations to be transported to the rear zone. All valuable materials, including non-ferrous metals, corn and fuel which cannot be taken away must be destroyed.

"In areas occupied by the enemy, guerilla detachments must be created as well as groups of saboteurs entrusted with fighting against the units of the enemy army, launching of guerilla warfare everywhere, blowing up bridges and roads, wrecking telephone and telegraph communications, and setting forests, depots and trains on fire. It is necessary to create in invaded areas conditions unbearable to the enemy."

SOVIET WOMANHOOD

THE women of Soviet Russia played an important part in their country's resistance to the invaders. It was not merely a passive part, but an active one, in keeping with the traditions of a country which boasted of the equality of opportunity accorded to its women. When the fall of Moscow seemed imminent the world learned of the total mobilization of the citizens affecting both sexes.

Russian women played their part in digging trenches at the approaches to the city; as in Britain they had replaced and added to male labour in the armament factories which provided troops on the Central Front with much of its supplies. As nurses they took their places in the front line, crawling under fire to minister to wounded Red Army men. In the city itself they stood patiently in queues to collect the barely sufficient food rations, braving the bombs and machine gun fire of German raiders.

In accordance with the policy of total resistance to total attack, many women of the Soviet Union trained themselves to use weapons, familiarizing themselves with the deadly craft of the sniper and machine-gunner. They practised throwing grenades and combating tanks, the women of the cities as well as those of the scattered towns, villages and hamlets.

Many Soviet women were honoured with decorations, but it is to the unknown millions of courageous, patient Natashas and Olgas that Russia owed much of her strength in the dark and desperate days of total warfare.

NO SHIRKING. *Russian women of all ages, all occupations, take picks and shovels to help in building defences.*

MOSCOW HOLDS OUT

"MOSCOW MADNESS" represents Hitler's attitude to the country in which he aped the part of Napoleon; as with the latter the battle for Moscow did more than anything else to ruin him. For here it was that, after overrunning nearly half the country, the German armies came to grief upon the stubborn, incalculable resistance of the Red Army.

Danger first threatened the city when, early in October, 1941, the oncoming Germans made a pincers thrust at it by the direct road from Smolensk and by way of the Valdai Hills. Marshal Timoshenko's armies were severely handled by immense numbers of tanks, aircraft and artillery. They were compelled to yield Orel, Vyazma and Briansk, but they burnt the villages as they retired and they fought for every town until it became a heap of rubble. But by the end of the month Moscow seemed doomed to fall.

Moscow Partially Evacuated

Roads radiate from Moscow in all directions. Kalinin on the north, Mojaisk on the west, Kaluga to the south-west, Tula to the south, form points all 60 to 70 miles away; up to and around these places the battle surged for many weeks in a vast semi-circle. Mid-October marked a crisis. The Government removed to Kuibyshev; important war factories were transported far to the east. Stalin, however, remained in the historic Kremlin, his presence acting as an inspiration to the defenders.

A tremendous A.A. barrage, greater than any seen before, was set up to cover the city, and this prevented the efforts of the enemy to annihilate the capital from having their desired effect.

Meanwhile the Germans thrust on down all the chief roads to Moscow, employing 49 divisions with many thousands of tanks and armoured vehicles and scores of thousands of lorries; while the Russians met them head on, their guerillas worried the enemy's rear and their Air Force strafed his communications. Nothing was abandoned without a struggle. Orel, for instance, was lost, recaptured, and lost again before the tide swept on to Tula; and so with Tula itself where a dangerous thrust by armoured cars was stopped only by the self-sacrifice of a handful of patriots.

British Help Arrives

Kalinin became a ghastly shambles, Germans firing from one half of the ruins, Russians from the other. At a critical hour British help arrived in the shape of many Valentine tanks and a wing of the R.A.F., the first of a steady flow of up-to-date war material; while from the east a constant stream of reinforcements—Siberian and Mongolian regiments, guns, tanks and ammunition—poured in to make losses good.

Finally "General Winter" began to take a hand. There had been early snow in October. Heavy frost followed and the Germans, in their confidence unprepared for winter weather, often perished miserably, whereas the Russian troops were warmly clad. By mid-November the situation was critical. Hitler had issued the order that Moscow *must* be taken at all costs; but although his armies had got within 40 miles of their objective they could not reach it.

The Germans became exhausted, and through the snows of January the

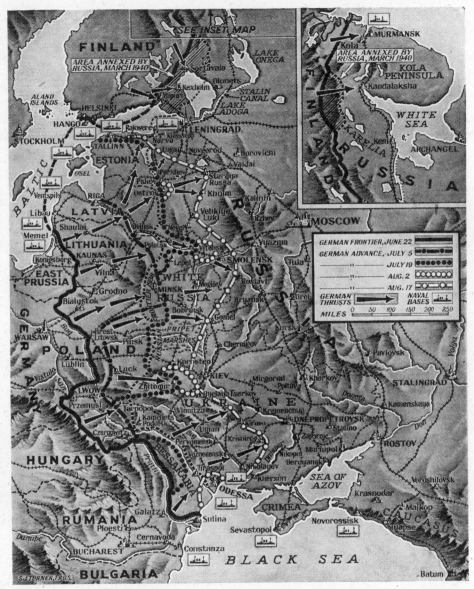

RUSSIA AT BAY. *Impetus of armoured German thrusts over Russia's frontier can be seen from the above map. The crucial sector was in the centre, approaching Moscow.*

Russians began to roll them back. Neither the weather nor the patriot army gave the invaders rest or pity. "The enemy," said Stalin, "has asked for a merciless war; he shall have it." How many men, how much material, was lost in the attack on Moscow may never be known. The Russians estimated that from the beginning of the great November drive to Christmas Day the Germans lost 127,000 men, 3,146 tanks, and quantities of material.

THE HARD WAY HOME. *A field piece drawn by starving horses, slipping and shivering as they picked their way along the snow-filled ruts and potholes of a Russian road ; a long column of men, huddled inside their cloaks in an effort to escape the biting wind—a typical scene during the German retreat during the hard winter of 1941.*

Forests that flanked the roads harboured bands of Russian guerillas, hating the invaders who had destroyed prosperity in the farmlands and cities of Soviet Russia. The German who incautiously strayed from his fellows found a bullet ; columns were ambushed. The way back was strewn with German dead and abandoned and wrecked equipment.

ATLANTIC MEETING

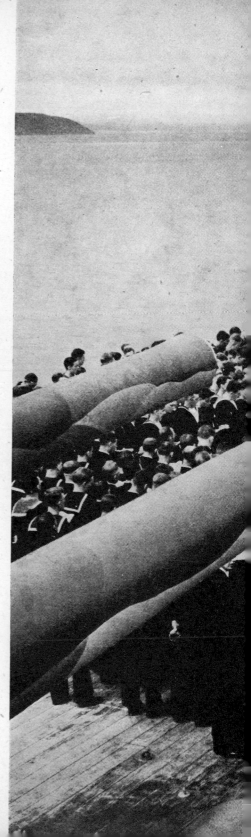

THE Atlantic Charter Meeting, held in August, 1941, showed President Roosevelt's clear perception, almost from the beginning of the war, that Hitlerism and all its implications involved the gravest danger to the American people.

The President reached the Atlantic rendezvous aboard the cruiser *Augusta*, and Mr. Churchill was aboard the new battleship *Prince of Wales*. Both men were accompanied by their Service and financial advisers, including Sir Dudley Pound, Sir John Dill, Sir Wilfred Freeman, Lord Beaverbrook, and Sir Alexander Cadogan on the British side, and Admirals King and Stark, General Marshall, Mr. Sumner Wells, Mr. Harry Hopkins, and Mr. Averell Harriman on the other. From the meeting emerged basic principles.

The points may be summarized as follows: No country shall interfere with the internal affairs of another or covet its territory. Those who have lost their rights through aggression shall be helped to regain them. All countries should have equal access to essential raw materials. Force should not be used to decide international affairs, and the peace should ensure freedom from want and freedom from fear, with international co-operation the aim.

During the meetings the party attended divine service one bright Sunday morning on board *Prince of Wales*. "The sun," said the Premier, in one of his brilliant war-time speeches, "shone bright and warm, while we sang the old hymns which are our common heritage."

"ONWARD, CHRISTIAN SOLDIERS."
This was one of the hymns sung during divine service on board Prince of Wales *attended by both Premier and President.*

HISTORIC MOMENT. *Franklin Delano Roosevelt, President of the United States, comes aboard H.M.S.* Prince of Wales *in August, 1941 to meet the Prime Minister,*

The President shakes hands warmly with Captain Leach, whilst Prime Minister Winston Churchill and British representatives smile at their distinguished guests.

ARK ROYAL LOST

NOVEMBER 14, 1941. The scene is early morning a few miles east of Gibraltar; the sea is grey and cold. A great ship lies in her death agony, like a huge whale lying on its side. Then she turns completely over and within a space of minutes has quietly sunk out of sight. No unusual spectacle this, in that year of U-boat sinkings all over the Western Ocean; but very unusual in that the victim was H.M.S. *Ark Royal*, pride of the Royal Navy and despair of the Germans.

Ark Royal, the first great modern aircraft carrier, was built in 1937. She carried 60 planes—Skuas, Swordfish, and eventually Fulmar Petrels, and most of these went down with her. Her war record had been magnificent, for she had steamed scores of thousands of miles, north towards Iceland, south to the Cape, west to Rio, east to Malta. In the first month of the war, while she was supporting battleships which were escorting a damaged submarine across the North Sea, a Heinkel 111 flew over her and dropped one huge bomb into the sea within thirty yards of the bow.

" Where is the Ark Royal ? "

The carrier rocked, but escaped. The pilot claimed an uncertain hit; but the chance was too good for the German propagandists to miss, so—on paper—they sank her and for months the German wireless asked, "Where is *Ark Royal*?" Their news service must have been bad, because she was everywhere. Her planes scoured the Norwegian fjords during the short British campaign there in 1940. She was at Iran, where her aircraft torpedoed *Dunkerque*. She sought out *Bismarck*, which her Swordfish dealt a mortal blow.

She convoyed merchantmen into Valetta, and she had so often attacked Sardinia that two of the ship's kittens were named Smash and Grab, the Cagliari twins. Whenever there was fighting, there you would find *Ark Royal*. After one action she had only seven airworthy planes. And now, after two years' glorious fighting, she was gone, fortunately with only one casualty among her large crew.

Unseen Death Blow

On that unlucky day, November 13, the ship had been out at exercises when an unseen submarine torpedoed her at about 4 a.m. on the starboard side, beneath the bridge. Internal communication ceased at once and she took a heavy list. Captain L. E. Maund had her engines stopped and water pumped into the other side so as to correct her trim. The destroyer *Legion* was called alongside, a dangerous job with the big ship hanging over her, and 1,540 of *Ark Royal's* crew were transferred to her crowded decks.

The destroyer *Laforey* improvised a power supply. In the bowels of the great ship volunteers worked frantically in the fume-laden stokeholds to raise steam from the flooded boilers. Oil ran along the sloping decks and caught fire repeatedly before being smothered.

Meanwhile the tugs had raced up from Gibraltar and an effort was made to tow the stricken giant to safety. The list was now so great that it was feared she would turn over and take her escorts down with her. It was decided to abandon ship. The gallant stokers slipped down into the sea, the captain was the last to leave. She rolled over on to her side until the flight deck

LAST MOMENTS OF *ARK ROYAL*. *Towering over the deck of the destroyer* Legion, *the torpedoed carrier,* Ark Royal, *is shown shortly before her final plunge. Smoke from burning oil eddies from her sides as the crew of about* 1,600 *clamber down to safety.*

stood vertically out of the water, then turned bottom up and made her final death plunge. So efficient and disciplined had been her crew during the last moments of the 23,000 ton carrier, that of her complement of about 1,600 officers and men, only one lost his life— an amazing feat of cool-headed seamanship. She was the third aircraft carrier to be lost since the war began.

It is noteworthy that four days before the communique announcing the sinking of *Ark Royal*, notice was issued

of the end of another famous, though much smaller, warship, whose spectacular career had in many ways paralleled the almost legendary exploits of the carrier. This was the destroyer *Cossack* (1,870 tons), which had rescued the British seamen from the prison-ship *Altmark*, daringly destroyed an enemy cruiser during the second battle of Narvik, and planted a torpedo in *Bismarck* during the famous Atlantic chase. Thus in one week two of the Royal Navy's famous ships had gone.

JAPANESE TREACHERY

PEARL HARBOUR has become a byword for treachery, but Japanese political deceit was already proverbial. The actual story is simple.

Soon after dawn on December 7, 1941, a large flight of planes was seen far out at sea, but owing to a combination of errors they were assumed to be friendly. Shortly after 8 a.m. Japanese torpedo-carrying aircraft and dive-bombers wheeled over the island. Some made for the air ports, others for the American fleet in the harbour.

Within half an hour there were 12 attacks. One ship turned right over and sank in the harbour, bottom up; others were ablaze or sinking; the oil tanks were belching black smoke; the airport hangars were in ruins and three-quarters of the air fleet, caught on the ground, had ceased to exist. Recovering

CAUGHT ON THE GROUND. *Explosions shroud the Naval Air Station at Pearl Harbour with smoke—grounded aircraft were unable to take off from their wrecked aerodrome. Three-quarters of the 202 naval planes were destroyed or damaged, besides 97 army aircraft: while of the army personnel 226 men were killed and 396 injured.*

from their first surprise the Americans hit back gallantly; some enemy planes were destroyed and two midget submarines which had penetrated into the harbour were captured.

But by this time the position had become hopeless. "It was just Hell let loose," said one observer, and by 9.30 when the Japanese pilots made off an incredible scene of destruction remained.

Probably no single air attack has had such an effect since. The 86 warships included 8 good battleships, every one of which was hit. Two were sunk (*Oklahoma* and *Arizona*) and three more seriously damaged. The old battleship *Utah*, used as a target ship, was destroyed. Two brand new cruisers, the older cruiser *Raleigh*, a new seaplane tender and a repair ship damaged. Three destroyers and a mine-layer were also total losses.

The effect of this air blitz was to paralyse American naval activity in the Pacific during the early months when Japan was sweeping across the whole of the south-west Pacific.

Ground staff and pilots fumed impotently by while the shrewdly planned attack encountered no opposition except that from the anti-aircraft batteries on the island. Although the Japanese benefited considerably from the results of this attack, it roused the inexorable determination of the angry American people to avenge it tenfold.

JAP WARPLANES TURN AWAY. *The American battleship* California *settles down into the muddy depths of Pearl Harbour as the Japanese airmen finish their attack.*

Clouds of smoke obscure the stricken American Fleet, caught unprepared by assault from bombs and torpedoes. Extreme right may be glimpsed the hulk of the Oklahoma.

WAR AGAINST JAPAN

ANGER, surprise and humiliation reigned at Washington when the news of the Pearl Harbour disaster was broken over the radio to the American people, but anger was the predominating emotion.

On December 8, the day after the attack, President Roosevelt's ringing tones denounced the act of treachery, made all the worse by the fact that even after the attack had begun Japan's representatives were discussing the future peaceful relationship of Japan and the U.S.A. with the American Secretary of State.

The President declared that, as Commander-in-Chief of his country's forces, he had taken all necessary steps for mobilization, adding: "I ask that the Congress declare that since the

AMERICA REPLIES. *President Roosevelt signs his country's declaration of war.*

unprovoked and dastardly attack by Japan on Sunday, December 7, 1941, a state of war has existed between the United States and the Japanese Empire. With confidence in our armed forces, with the unbounded determination of the people, we will gain the inevitable triumph, so help us God." The answer of Congress was immediate. Except for a single Pacifist vote, both houses voted for war unanimously and without discussion.

In Britain Mr. Churchill announced that the Japanese had begun a landing in British territory in Northern Malaya the previous day, and that the Royal Netherlands Government had informed Japan that as the result of the hostile acts against Britain and America a state of war existed between the Kingdom of the Netherlands and Japan.

Mr. Churchill closed his address with a tribute to the people of China: "the House will remember that both I and the Foreign Secretary had felt able to make increasingly outspoken declarations of friendship for the Chinese people and their great leader, General Chiang Kai-shek. We have always been friends. Last night I cabled the General-issimo assuring him that henceforward we would fight the common foe together. . . . When we think of the insane ambition and insatiable appetite which have caused this vast and melancholy extension of the war, we can only feel that Hitler's madness has infected the Japanese mind and the roots of the evil and its branch must be extirpated together."

The reaction of the British Empire was immediate and inspiring. Australia was particularly menaced, and the Prime Minister, Mr. Curtin, broadcast: "Our forces are at their battle

NEVER-TO-BE-FORGOTTEN SCENE. *Graven into the minds of millions of Americans was the scene of destruction at Pearl Harbour—emblem of Japanese treachery.*

stations. I give the assurance that the Australian Government is fully prepared. We will hold this country and keep it as a citadel of the British-speaking race." In New Zealand, Mr. Peter Frazer, outlining emergency measures, concluded: "The people of Britain have set us a noble example; we will live up to it, come what may." Canada and South Africa joined the chorus of condemnation and fierce determination which Japan's sudden entry into the arena of the Second World War had provoked.

In a long and emotional speech Hitler welcomed his new comrades in arms, announcing that Germany had added the United States to her list of enemies. He launched a violent attack on the President and Mrs. Roosevelt, accusing them of insanity, corruption, and increasing the American national debt. "Behind me is the National Socialist Party, with which I grew great and which grew great with me and by me. I thank the President, I thank God, for the opportunity given to me and to the German nation."

PACIFIC DISASTER

CONFIDENCE in Britain received a severe shaking when, within 48 hours of Japan's attack on Malaya, news came that the brand-new battleship *Prince of Wales* (35,000 tons) and the old, but serviceable, battle-cruiser *Repulse* (sister ship of famous *Renown*) had been sunk.

A few weeks earlier these ships had been sent East to reinforce the small naval force at Singapore. They should have been supported by an aircraft carrier, but *Ark Royal* had just gone to the bottom, and the few other modern carriers were either under repair or elsewhere engaged.

On December 8, 1941, Admiral Phillips, flying his flag on *Prince of Wales*, received a message that Japanese transports were attempting landings on the east coast of Malaya. He had to decide whether to remain beneath Singapore's air cover or to attack. He chose the latter course and set out boldly to intercept the enemy transports.

Finding no trace of the enemy, he decided at dusk to turn back. He had with him *Repulse* and some destroyers. Enemy reconnaissance had picked out this small squadron and on the 10th both battleships were assailed by a shower of bombs and aerial torpedoes.

After three hours the Admiral signalled his consort and learned that so far *Repulse* had avoided 19 torpedoes. Then another swarm of aircraft came over, diving from all quarters with complete disregard of casualties.

Repulse, hit repeatedly, sank. Then *Prince of Wales*, hit in four or five places, went down after her. It was all over in half an hour and all the destroyer escort could do was to pick up casualties. Both the Admiral, and his Flag Captain were amongst those

TRAGEDY AT SEA. *The tragic last moments of the stricken* Prince of Wales.

who perished. Thus the Japanese dealt the Allies a resounding blow in the first stages of the struggle for the Pacific.

Prince of Wales had a short but adventurous history. The second British giant 4-turret battleship, she had been slightly damaged during the chase of *Bismarck*. It was this ship, too, that carried Winston Churchill to Maine,

Seamen swarm along ropes attached to the light rescue vessels who have raced up to her side. Those of her crew awaiting the chance to escape preserve perfect discipline.

when, with President Roosevelt, he drafted the terms of the Atlantic Charter. She was also the first British capital ship to succumb to enemy air attack in any operational zone.

Repulse (32,000 tons) was one of the class of battle-cruisers launched in 1916. After serving in the First World War she was reconditioned, although by

modern standards her construction and design possessed several weaknesses.

The loss of two capital ships in the Pacific, combined with the damage done to the American Fleet at Pearl Harbour, altered the balance of sea power in the Far East, giving Japan temporary mastery enhanced by her numerical superiority in the air.

HONG KONG FALLS

WHEN Japan attacked the Democracies the position of Hong Kong was desperate. The little island, with its large population and small water supply, could not possibly stand a siege; while the hills guarding the approach from the mainland required an army, not a few battalions, for adequate defence. There was virtually no air support, and only a few small warships at sea.

The enemy launched their first attack on the morning after the Pearl Harbour raid, their planes twice bombing the island besides machine-gunning Kowloon on the mainland opposite. Within 24 hours the mainland was attacked and nothing but a retreat to the island remained. On December 14, the Governor, Sir Mark Young, rejected a summons to surrender and across the narrow straits British and Japanese guns barked defiance at each other. Faced with a situation which could end only in defeat, the Governor addressed his last

message to the troops : " Be strong, be resolute, and do your duty." The Japanese were pouring across like a horde of warrior ants, methodically splitting the defenders into small parties. Counter attacks were made, many individual epics of heroism were recorded, while the crowded native population of this over-populated island met constant air attacks with the patient stoicism of their kind.

Gradually the inexhaustible pressure of the enemy squeezed the city tighter, until British, Canadian and Indian troops held only a ring round the mountainous core of Hong Kong. Then came the crowning calamity—the reservoirs were captured. With only one day's water remaining the Governor applied for a truce. After a long argument with the Japanese he surrendered. It was then Christmas Day. The photograph shows the entry of the Japanese Forces into the city. The victors—inspired by the spirit of " Bushido," their name for chivalry— bound fifty officers and men and allowed their troops to bayonet them.

VOICES OF DEMOCRACY

HISTORY was made on December 26, 1941, when Winston Churchill addressed United States Congress. He dealt with the great tasks of the United Nations :

"The forces ranged against us are enormous. They are bitter, they are ruthless. The wicked men and their factions who have launched their peoples on the path of war and conquest know that they will be called to terrible account if they cannot beat down by force of arms the people they have assailed. . . . They will stop at nothing that violence or treachery suggests. . . I avow my hope and faith, sure and inviolate, that in the days to come the British and American peoples will . . . walk together in majesty, in justice, and in peace."

President Roosevelt added his voice in these inspiring words: "The present over-all objective is the marshalling of all resources, military and economic, of

PRIME MINISTER. *Symbolic of the new comradeship between the peoples of the British Empire and the United States was Mr. Churchill's address before America's Congress.*

PRESIDENT. *Three times elected President of the U.S.A., Mr. Roosevelt welcomed the close collaboration between the two great democracies, in peace as well as time of war.*

the world-wide front opposing the Axis. Excellent progress along these lines is being made. . . . Through brute force and enslavement Hitler has secured a measure of integration and co-ordination of the productive forces of a large part of Europe; we must demonstrate that the integration and co-ordination of the productive forces of America are possible through democratic process and free consent."

On January 1, 1942 a further step was taken when 26 nations at war with Italy, Germany, and Japan issued from Washington a declaration of co-operation in the struggle. Each Government pledged itself to "employ its full resources, military and economic, against those members of the Tripartite Pact and its adherents with which such a Government is at war." Henceforth the economic and military plans of the United Nations were to be co-ordinated as a mighty, awe-inspiring whole.

FAR EAST. *Above is shown progress of the war against Japan up to the enemy seizure of the Andaman Islands, which took place on March 23, 1942. It will be seen that the whole of Malaya had been overrun, and Borneo, Java, and Celebes had been occupied. The gallant American and Filipino Forces were still hanging on in the Philippines, though their resistance was to prove unavailing. From their foothold on New Guinea, the enemy were menacing Australia. Here they were eventually halted.*

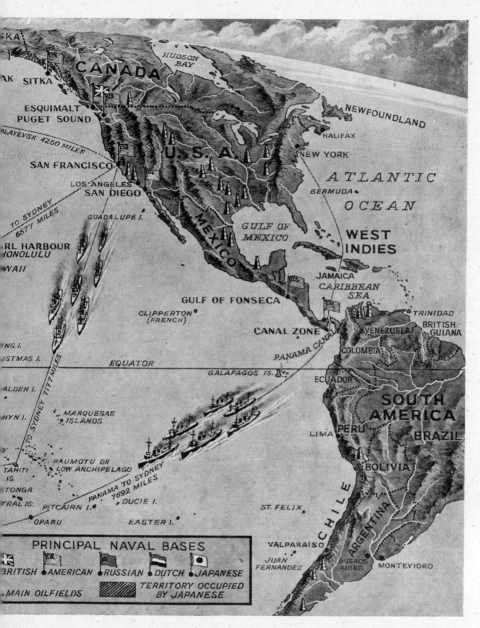

PRINCIPAL NAVAL BASES

BRITISH · AMERICAN · RUSSIAN · DUTCH · JAPANESE

MAIN OILFIELDS · TERRITORY OCCUPIED BY JAPANESE

Before the impetus of the Japanese tide was stemmed it was to overrun most of the numerous Pacific islands, each one of which was to be recaptured when the Allied war effort got into its stride. But as the situation stood in the March of 1942 the Japanese position looked extremely strong. The Far Eastern supply line with Russia was cut, and shipping in the Indian Ocean threatened. The enemy seemed about to seal off China from all outside help, and to advance on India through the Burmese jungles.

TRAGEDY OF SINGAPORE

THE Singapore disaster, in essence, was the same as that of Hong Kong; too little of everything except self-confidence on the one side, too much of everything on the other. Singapore itself lies on an island, about the size and shape of the Isle of Wight, but flat, the town and naval station facing the mainland. The Malay Peninsula itself could only be defended by a large army with abundant armour and sufficient aircraft.

As it was the British, Australians and Indians never mustered more than six gallant, hard-fighting divisions. They had no armour, and mostly old planes —some Hurricanes had been rushed there, but most of them were still in crates when Singapore finally fell.

Shortly after midnight on December 7, 1941—before they declared war—the enemy sent transports and warships stealing across the Siamese Gulf. Some made for the northern airport at Khota Bharu, which they seized; others got astride the isthmus, thus making it impracticable to advance up both coasts at once.

Jungle Tactics

Skilled in jungle fighting, singularly well provided with maps, the invaders would climb trees, drop bombs therefrom on their opponents, and disappear. On the east coast more and more lightly equipped Japanese appeared, while the loss of *Prince of Wales* and *Repulse* made the task of the defenders far harder. Slowly the Allied troops were forced back south, burning the country behind them. The enemy adopted the policy of infiltrating behind the opposing lines, making continuous withdrawals necessary. They did not accomplish this unscathed. At Negri Sembilan and Muar the Australians, their blood aroused, mauled the Japanese badly, but the end of January saw the mainland abandoned altogether.

This left the British commander at Singapore in an untenable position. His 70,000 men were separated from the enemy by a shallow river only; he could be taken in the rear at any point, and he had behind him a city of a million souls. Singapore was not a fortress but a naval station; its defences faced out to sea, for no one had envisaged a land attack.

Final Surrender

Singapore was bombed repeatedly and wantonly; by day and night the sirens wailed; heroic Chinese bandaged the wounded and cleared up the increasing mass of debris. Out to the north, only a few miles away, lay a cloud of smoke and the ground rocked to the thunder of guns. The causeway joining the island to the mainland was broken, but at the western edge of the city is a marshland and here and there the enemy managed to get across by night. As at Hong Kong the precious water supply was lost to the enemy and the scene darkened on one of the worst British military disasters in history. The reservoirs were so badly damaged that by February 14 only enough water remained to supply the million people of Singapore for one day.

The end was not long delayed; as at Hong Kong there came negotiations and finally surrender on February 15, 1942 followed by the spate of Japanese brutality as the Mikado's swaggering troops entered the city that for so long had been a symbol of British commerce and power in this part of the Orient.

JAPANESE TRIUMPH. *These small Japanese tanks are seen rolling over Singapore Causeway soon after the garrison's unconditional surrender on February 15, 1942.*

MALTA'S EPIC ENDURANCE

WHEN Italy declared war the Axis must have calculated that the fall of the islands of Malta would be one of the first results of their Mediterranean pressure. The islands, situated between Sicily and North Africa, possessed little A.A. defence, four sea Gladiator fighters in crates awaiting shipment to Alexandria, and a large civilian population to be looked after. But under the energetic command of General Sir William Dobbie and his successor, Lord Gort, the islands did hold out until the collapse of Italy removed the danger.

In the latter stages of the Mediterranean fighting the "aircraft carrier" that was Malta was a constant thorn in the side of the Axis strategists.

In the beginning the four Gladiators,

WHAT AXIS AIRMEN SAW. *As they came in over Malta from the sea, Axis airmen saw this peaceful panorama stretching beneath them as they endeavoured to destroy it.*

piloted by men unaccustomed to fighter warfare, took the air against squadrons of the Italian Air Force. One Gladiator was shot down, the other three battled on for three months until a Hurricane squadron arrived from Britain.

The civil population stood up to constant air raids. Dockyard workers helped man the defences; old tunnels were adapted as shelters; the Maltese rivalled the people of London in unostentatious bravery backed by hard work under fire.

And as German and Italian aeroplanes flew sortie after sortie the strength and usefulness of Malta grew apace. From her shelter naval squadrons fell upon enemy convoys, damaged vessels put into her dockyards for temporary repairs. Time and again the position of the islands verged upon desperation, but on each occasion supplies and reinforcements were got through. And on April 15, 1942, King George signed the award of the George Cross to the Island Fortress.

Four obsolescent Gladiators stood up to the daily raids until a Hurricane squadron arrived from England. In the end it was Italy who cracked and ignominiously gave up.

CORAL SEA BATTLE

WHAT was claimed to be the greatest naval engagement since Jutland, in 1916, took place between May 4-8, 1942, in the vicinity of the Solomon Islands, about 1,000 miles from Queensland.

It marked a turning point in the war against Japan; it was a sea battle in which all the damage was accomplished by aircraft.

In March, Australian and American aircraft had attacked enemy transports preparing to attack Port Moresby and Australia. By April the enemy had reorganized and the stage was set.

On May 4 a task force of the U.S. Pacific Fleet under Rear-Admiral Frank J. Fletcher, found part of the Japanese invasion Fleet at Tulagi (Solomons) and almost completely annihilated it, enemy losses amounting to 12 ships sunk or damaged and six aircraft destroyed.

This was only the prelude. Three days later Rear-Admiral Fletcher's warplanes struck again, this time at the main body of the Japanese fleet in the Coral Sea. Fifteen bombs and six tor-

pedoes tore the sides of the Jap carrier *Ryukaku*, which plunged down with almost all her planes still aboard. In addition an enemy cruiser was sunk and 25 aircraft shot out of the sky for the loss of only six American.

Thinking attack the best means of defence, the Japanese hurled their planes into the battle. On May 7 an American tanker was sunk, and the destroyer *Sims* went down with her. Most of the crew were saved. Next day the 33,000 ton U.S. ship, *Lexington*, originally a battle cruiser but now adapted as a carrier, blew up after hits

by several bombs and torpedoes. Over 90 per cent. of her crew escaped.

The Americans struck back, leaving another enemy carrier belching smoke and fire.

In cold figures the profit and loss account of the battle read: Japanese losses, 15 ships, including one carrier, 3 heavy cruisers, one light cruiser, and 2 destroyers: American losses, one aircraft carrier and one destroyer.

Last moments of *Lexington* are depicted in the above photograph, blazing with fire from her ruptured petrol tanks, and heeling over into the water.

167

AUSTRALIAN GUNNERS OPEN UP. *A scene in the Egyptian desert during the critical summer months of 1942 shows stalwart Australian gunners opening fire.*

THE EIGHTH AT BAY

JULY and AUGUST, 1942, were critical days for the defence of Egypt, a defence upon which turned the entire Middle East strategy of the Allied powers. Not since the days before General Wavell had smashed the first Italian threat had Britain's North African foothold seemed so precarious. This time the menace was not wholly Italian, for the Allies were faced by some of the hardest units in the German army, supported by a tremendous weight of armour, and led by the tough Nazi general Rommel, a man quick to seize and exploit any weakness in Allied strategy to the fullest extent.

Retreat to Egypt

After titanic battles between tanks at Knightsbridge, Acroma and Bir Hakeim, the British with most of their armour destroyed, contemplated making a determined stand at the Halfaya escarpment. An unexpected blow came when Tobruk, which was once more left to fend for itself with 28,000 men and considerable supplies, fell in a single day. The result of this was that a retreat into Egypt became imperative. At Mersa Matruh, a bleak little port on the edge of the desert, General Auchinleck, who had by now taken over the direct command of the British armies, ordered a temporary halt; in addition the bulk of his available forces were withdrawn 150 miles further to the partially constructed lines at El Alamein, only 60 miles away from Alexandria. Meanwhile Africa became first priority for supplies. Especially was the need for tanks and anti-tank guns of paramount urgency if Egypt was to be saved. Rommel, thinking that the game was now "in the bag," pursued vigorously,

and without a pause hurled his panzer divisions at the desert flank of the defenders, his intention being to drive them to the sea. This part of the line was held mainly by New Zealanders, who magnificently beat off five successive attacks, and then, although surrounded, charged through the enemy with the bayonet and regained the main body. The net closed, but Rommel found very little in it apart from burning dumps and wreckage left by the retreating British.

There followed a general mêlée between pursuers and pursued. Fortunately the Royal Air Force was now predominant, and by screaming down on to the enemy's transport and tanks, machine-gunning and bombing them without rest, they enabled a more or less orderly retreat to be made.

General Auchinleck's Message

The Eighth Army had no sooner reached Alamein than it was attacked by the panzer spearheads. The half-formed trenches were literally the last ditch; a break-through would have spelled disaster. But the enemy were beaten off. "You are fighting the Battle of Egypt," said General Auchinleck to his men, "a battle in which the enemy must be destroyed. You have shown that you can stick it, and I know you will stick it right out." They did stick it out, forcing Rommel to make a withdrawal and dig in. At this hour General Auchinleck himself was a tower of strength.

Jubilation reigned in Berlin. Rommel became the hero of the hour and made boastful statements concerning his future advances. Mussolini, overjoyed at seeing his fortunes on the way to recovery, caused medals to be struck commemorating the fall of Egypt and prepared to visit Cairo and Alexandria in state. And so throughout July the two armies, while preparing for the struggle that must come, skirmished spasmodically for certain ground—so-called ridges—which gave some slight advantage. The British were now near their base, whereas the enemy had a long supply line which was regularly blasted by the British bombers.

Alexander and Montgomery

One great petrol store established by the enemy at Mersa Matruh was fired and destroyed soon after it had been established and the toll of enemy transports became very severe. So the long, stifling days passed into August, marked by sandstorms and sniping.

General Alexander became Commander-in-Chief, with General Montgomery at the head of the indomitable Eighth Army. The new chief's orders were plain and precise: "There must be no further withdrawals, none at all, absolutely none whatever." He insisted on the closest liaison with the R.A.F. and his will to win was an inspiration. He was helped by important supplies of guns, tanks and spares; of men the desert could never accommodate more than a modest number.

By the end of August, Rommel, now short of oil, issued orders for an advance on Cairo. On the last day of the month he struck at the desert flank, a small space between the British and the morass. Some of his tanks got stuck in the quicksands; the rest, after boring into British minefields, were stopped before entrenchments and the muzzles of 25-pounders. In the middle of it all the R.A.F. ventured out in a violent sandstorm and pounded German lorry concentrations. The Germans lingered uncertainly among the minefields for several days, reluctant

THE CHASE IS ON. *With the last German bid smashed, Allied tanks move up.*

to give up, but unable to proceed. They then retired, holding on to one gain, the hill of Himeimat. The second assault on Egypt had failed. The most serious loss sustained by the Afrika Korps was in its armoured strength. Totally destroyed were 63 tanks, and others were more or less seriously damaged.

The defeat was explained away by the Germans as having been merely a reconnaissance in force. But Rommel

Montgomery's seasoned veterans were to chase the Afrika Korps across the arid expanses of the western desert, crushing the vestiges of Axis power in North Africa.

had issued an Order of the Day containing the following sentence: "To-day the Army, reinforced by new divisions, will launch a new attack in order finally to destroy the enemy."

The reasons for Rommel's failure were not hard to find. Firstly, the British had got the measure of the German tactics, which tended to repeat themselves. Secondly, in the words of General Freyburg, the Germans had become "tank followers" and had "lost their old skill in handling their personal weapons." Lastly, the morale of the British troops had been amazingly high, and the handling and repair of tanks greatly improved.

Thereafter Rommel was never able to recover the initiative, which henceforth was held firmly in the hands of the Allied generals until the Afrika Korps ceased to exist.

SEVASTOPOL

UNTIL the fateful battle of Stalingrad, the siege of Sevastopol was the greatest defensive action of the war. This naval base, home of the Russian Black Sea Fleet, was a constant threat to the German right flank, and guarded the port of Batum and the rich oil-bearing regions south of the Caucasus Mountains. Its capture became the highest priority in the German plan to knock out Russia.

Since the previous November, the Germans had established themselves in the Crimean Peninsula and invested the town. Their drive was backed by 100,000 first-class troops, hundreds of tanks and dive-bombers, and siege guns of new design. They had thought to blast a way through Sevastopol's defences by sheer weight of metal.

It was now June, 1942, and thousands of German troops had been fed into what had become a slaughter-house. In spite of the amount of high explosive

showered on them, the Red Army men, reinforced by marines of the Black Sea Fleet, continued to hold off the enemy. Their hardships were shared by many civilians who had refused evacuation and remained behind to play their part in the resistance. Then came the final, all-out German onslaught, delivered on a garrison short of many weapons, and weakened by months of ceaseless action.

On June 13, Fort Stalin, one of the key Russian strongpoints, fell after hand-to-hand fighting. Other attacks, made regardless of losses, were launched against Forts Maxim Gorki and Lenin. No hope of relief was now left, but isolated and outnumbered groups continued to fight. It was not until July 3 that the Germans were able to claim resistance at an end.

The photograph shows the extent of the devastation; nothing is left except the shells of buildings, and piles of wreckage, earth, and rubble. A few civilians are seen searching for food.

NEAR TOBRUK. *In the haze of the open desert British armoured cars are shown nearing Tobruk, supporting infantry as the battle for the western desert progresses.*

PART FOUR
TRIUMPH OF UNITED NATIONS

THE summer of 1942 marked the high water mark of Axis aggression. Gradually the military tide was to turn against the aggressors and in favour of the Allies, until by the summer of 1944 it was rushing back towards Germany and Japan, with the wretched Italy already submerged.

Africa, Russia and New Guinea, regions miles apart, were the places where the trend first became apparent. The massive Anglo-American counterblows, made possible by the endurance of the British Eighth Army, were to sweep the Axis from Africa ; at Stalingrad the flower of the German Army was to perish ; in New Guinea Australians and Americans were to administer the first of many decisive defeats to the forces of Japan.

The way to victory was a long hard climb from these significant initial successes, and it was only made possible by the efforts of millions of civilian workers in Britain, the Dominions, the United States and Russia. The way into the Continent could not have been forced, the Red Army's sweep through Poland and the continued blows against Japan in the Pacific would not have been possible without new, modern weapons forged in quantities that would have seemed impossible twenty years previously.

The Axis master-plan had been conceived on a grand scale. It envisaged the linking up of Germany, Italy and Japan in the East, through Russia or via Burma, Northern India, Afghanistan and Persia; with infiltration into South America and the isolation of North America as subse-

quent stages. This plan was to a certain extent fulfilled, but the Axis failed on the last lap.

At the conference table, the Allies had formulated their own plan for concerted world action. In the West their growing air strength pounded German industry, with every increasing stroke weakening the power of the enemy to hit back and paving the way towards the invasion of France. The Germans were powerless to prevent their ally, Italy, from invasion. Faced with the might of the United States Navy and other Allied units, the Japanese Navy failed in its task of keeping Japan's supply lines open to her newly conquered acquisitions. Unable to expand, the Axis Empire began to contract, the road back being rendered fearsome by the hatred of nations for so long held captive.

Success was not bought cheaply. The beaches of Anzio, Tarawa, and Normandy, the towns of Catania, Stalingrad and Kharkov, were won by the bravery of thousands of men, of many different languages and religions, but with one thing in common—hatred of aggression and all that it stood for. It was to nameless millions that the world owed its deliverance from the great peril.

And so, in the following pages the picture will unfold of Axis reverses and Allied triumphs. The path of totalitarianism to the brink of victory has been unfolded in previous pages ; now the dividing line has been reached and the spectacle is one of the triumph of the freedom-loving nations over those whose philosophy was one of violence.

DIRECT HIT. *Bursting shells from A.A. guns festoon the air with balls of smoke as a Japanese bomber registers a direct hit upon U.S.A. aircraft carrier Yorktown.*

MIDWAY

Japanese losses far outnumbered those of the Allies in this decisive action on the sea.

THIS was the heaviest defeat sustained by the Japanese up till June, 1942 The enemy had overrun the whole of the Netherlands East Indies, advances had been made on New Guinea, and an effort had been made to seize Port Moresby as an air base for a descent upon Northern Australia, which, thanks largely to the reckless heroism of the R.A.A.F had been smashed

Then powerful Japanese naval units, protected by aircraft carriers. sailed from Japan for Midway Island America's lonely little outpost in mid ocean, far west of Hawaii and almost midway between San Francisco and Tokio. The island had been attacked unsuccessfully four times before, and on this occasion the enemy intended the massed blow to be decisive. They hoped to catch the defences unprepared, but not only had shore forces and A.A. batteries been reinforced, but Admiral Nimitz had a strong task force of the U.S. Navy to hand, with air cover.

The enemy armada comprised at least 80 ships. Aircraft were flown off its numerous carriers, the 26,000-ton *Akagi* and *Kaga*, and various smaller ships. They were met by American fighters and a heavy barrage and the majority of their bombs fell wide. Meanwhile planes from the giant American carrier *Yorktown* descended upon the enemy fleet, sinking the 10,000-ton carrier *Hiryu*.

As the Japanese withdrew, *Yorktown* was put out of action and a destroyer sunk. But the Americans sank the small carrier *Soryu*, together with the *Akagi* and *Kaga*, and downed 275 planes. Two enemy heavy cruisers were sunk, and three damaged, besides three destroyers and four transports.

THE ADVANCE BEGINS

THE third struggle for El Alamein is one of the world's outstanding battles. When it began, on October 23, 1942, Rommel's army was astride a tremendously strong trench system, with gun pits and mines, all intended to pin down the British until they could be driven into the Nile. When it ended, that proud force was a fugitive rabble, running for shelter where none was to be had, or crying piteously for water.

After the failure of his August attack, Rommel took warning and himself went to Berlin to ask 'or reinforcements; but he got very little, and he returned only in time to find the battle already on, and to take over when his deputy was captured.

General Montgomery had long planned this attack. Weeks before the August battle he had pointed out to Mr Churchill and General Alexander that recent desert tactics must be reversed, and he obtained approval then of his scheme 'or achieving victory. Part of the Eighth Army, to be called the Xth Corps, was to be withdrawn and intensively trained behind the lines; it would be heavily armoured. At the right moment 25-pounders, spaced only 23 yards apart over a distance of 6,000 yards, would smother the enemy's batteries in the north, near the sea. Behind the barrage infantry would advance and force a gap; and when the gap had been made —then and then only—the Xth Corps would be hurled into it like a thunderbolt, to roll the enemy up in ruin.

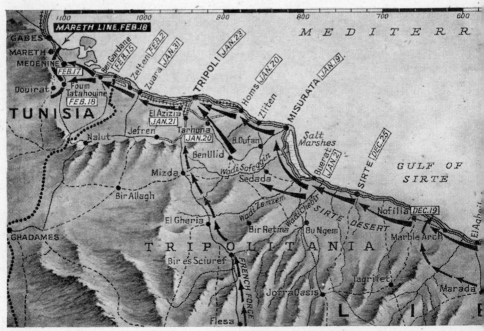

DRIVE THROUGH TRIPOLITANIA. *Rapidity of the Eighth's advance from El Alamein commencing November 1, 1942, is shown in successive stages on this map.*

Zero hour was to be 9.40 p.m. on October 23, 1942, when the troops would be helped by a full moon. Unlike most plans of battle, moreover, this one operated to the letter. Its success was helped by an admirable trick, the Xth Corps silently decamping towards the front, but leaving its tents and lines behind to deceive the enemy's aircraft.

The minefields were cleared at two points; then came that tremendous barrage. Such was the effect of the guns that the Germans were stunned and bewildered, and within a few hours our infantry had pushed forward three miles and had gained their first objectives. Beyond lay a slight rise, called Kidney Ridge, and beyond that El Aqqakir, where most of Rommel's armour lay. On the British right, across the railway, the 9th Australian Brigade attacked formidable German forces and also made good progress. In the British centre, Indian and other troops began to force the Germans off the last remaining bit they held of Ruweisat Ridge; and in the south, Free French attacked Hemeimat. These inland blows, though really feints, were strong enough to hold up the enemy and divert his attention. Overhead the R.A.F. provided perfect co-operation, following the troops, breaking up enemy transport and tanks, and once dispersing a threatened blow by many panzers and leaving them wrecked.

There was a long struggle to maintain the two gaps, which were now in the middle of the German defence system; but everything gained was held, and day after day the hammering continued. Out on the coast the Australians pinned part of the enemy to a strong point and passed on,

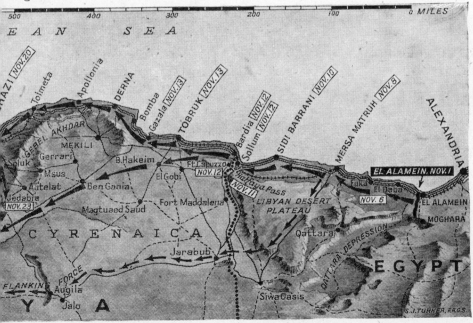

El Agheila, on the Gulf of Sirte, was the place where the Afrika Korps were expected to make a backs-to-the-wall stand, but this port fell to the Eighth on December 13.

leaving the Germans enclosed in their rear. At Kidney Ridge the 2nd Rifle Brigade covered itself with glory, and its leader, Lieut.-Colonel V. B. Turner, earned the V.C. by holding ground it had seized against 100 tanks throughout a whole day; 55 of the tanks were put out of action. After eight days of this ding-dong struggle, Rommel had reason to think that the battle was dying down, when, at 2.0 a.m. on November 2, another terrific creeping barrage rolled forward towards Aqqakir. The German batteries were blasted to pieces. Through the gap infantry poured; and then, just at the right moment, General Freyberg led the armoured might of the Xth Corps through, and in a furious tank battle around Aqqakir knocked out 250 of the enemy; 200 German guns were also wrecked. By the 3rd, victory was ours; by the 4th the enemy was in disorderly retreat. His Italian allies, shut in between the Qattara morass and the British, were abandoned to their fate.

Confusion quickly led to chaos, and the retreat became a rout. The Rommel bubble of invincibility had been burst.

By the afternoon of November 3, General Montgomery found it possible to issue the following message to the men who had fought so stubbornly and well: "The present battle has lasted 12 days, during which all troops have fought so magnificently that the enemy is being worn down.

"He has just reached breaking point, and he is trying to get his army away. The R.A.F. is taking heavy toll of his columns moving west on the main coast road. . . .

"I call on all troops to keep up the pressure and not relax one moment. We have the chance of putting the whole panzer army in the bag.

"I congratulate all troops on what has been achieved. Complete victory is almost in sight. On your behalf I have sent a separate message to the R.A.F., thanking them for their quite magnificent effort."

" THANKS, ROMMEL ! " *Welcome cover has been found by these British troops— behind the remains of an abandoned German tank. They open fire with a Bren gun.*

THE EIGHTH GOES IN TO ATTACK. *The long duel between the German Afrika Korps and the British Eighth Army provided one of the great stories of the war. This photograph shows men of the Eighth charging in to attack during the outflanking drive to Nufilia, which entailed moving their supplies over almost impassable country.*

" HIT FOR SIX "

" THE Boche," said General Montgomery, on the morrow of El Alamein, " is completely finished. The road behind is blocked with stuff four deep trying to get away. We intend to hit this chap for six right out of Africa."

This was no mere boast. The hit, in fact, had been made, and the human ball was on its way, helped by a hail of bombs from above, and surrounded by the wreckage of his armour and the smell of burning transport. Having one road, and no air cover, the fleeing Germans and Italians suffered as the civilians of Belgium and France had in 1940; they had shown no pity and they got none now. Neither rain, nor dust, nor sandstorms, nor desperate efforts of brave groups of rearguards— for the German rearguards were at times heroic—could ward off the pursuit or slacken it for more than a moment.

At the very start the British got ahead and near El Daba the enemy tanks ran into a trap and were still more depleted. Up the only road to the Libyan plateau, by famed Halfaya Pass, the enemy struggled, with but a single thought, to get away. The black mass of men and vehicles, halted around bomb craters, formed a perfect mark for the British artillery, which was not slow to shell it; nor did they halt on the plateau, but fled past El Adem, Knightsbridge, Gazala, all the famous names of desert battle grounds, to their strong point at Mersa Brega, just east of El Agheila, the port on the Gulf of Sirte which they had to abandon.

MEN IN CAGES. *Axis troops behind wire fences react in different ways. Some seem stunned, others seem to be resigned.*

TALLY HO ! *Tanks move up during the Alamein offensive. The armoured columns of Rommel's army are falling back as Allied reinforcements move up into the battle area.*

Here, between the marshes and the sea, a stand was possible. The South Africans swooped aside to recapture Tobruk; the main force occupied Benghazi once more. By this time 30,000 prisoners had been counted, including 9 generals, and the enemy had not a score of his original tanks left; but still the tireless conqueror urged on the pursuit. "Our task is not yet finished," ran his order. "On with the task, and good hunting to you!"

At El Agheila came a pause, while the Eighth Army gathered momentum, and its transport officers did un-

believable things in bringing up supplies, for Montgomery would not sacrifice men on any headstrong venture. When he was ready, December 13, Mersa Brega was neatly turned on both flanks; and Rommel withdrew again by rapid stages across the lonely desert coast road to Tripoli. Deep rocky wadis and other obstacles there were, but he could not defend them because he lacked the strength. Ninety miles beyond Agheila a brilliant march through the swamps placed the British van across the line of retreat, and the Eighth Army bit off the German tail.

Clouds of smoke and dust from shell bursts overhang this dramatic scene. The tank commanders stand on the turrets to direct gunfire at the distant enemy positions.

By Christmas Day the Union flag had reached Sirte. At Wadi Zemzem one panzer division made a half-hearted stand; but the position, naturally formidable, was easily carried. The enemy passed right through Tripoli without stopping; and then at last, at 5.0 a.m. on January 23, 1943, the head of the Eighth Army entered the city. It had covered 1,350 miles in 80 days, including many fights. The Italian African empire had ceased to exist.

Since the first attack at El Alamein the Eighth Army had advanced over some of the most difficult campaigning country in the world. The provision of water, food, ammunition, parts required for repairs, medical services, and the thousand and one things needed by an army in battle had been an astonishing feat of military organization. No less amazing was the physical endurance shown by the men who had fought battle after battle against some of Germany's best troops and commanders.

Italy was left to lament the loss of regions "that have belonged to us for a third of a century." In Berlin silence reigned as the Germans counted their losses in the months of disaster.

AFRICAN LANDING

News of the loss of Tobruk reached Mr. Churchill in Washington at the moment when, in conjunction with President Roosevelt, he was planning a descent upon North Africa that would finally eject the Axis from that continent; despite the setback all plans went ahead in November, 1942.

The project was ambitious. At the outset a quarter of a million men and one million tons of stores were to be landed at several more or less hostile ports up to four thousand miles away from America. Even if the French did not oppose the landings, it was certain that the expedition would be harassed continually by U-boats and ocean-ranging aircraft. The organisation alone was to be a gigantic task, involving elaborate shipping schedules, study of tides and beaches, selection of the right ships, provision of naval escorts, and particular attention to proper stowage of cargo. As the expedition was American, General Dwight Eisenhower became its head, but under him the British provided a large contingent —the First Army, commanded by General Anderson.

The naval arrangements were organised mainly by Admiral Sir Bertram Ramsay, the Americans providing their own escort for the part which sailed direct from the U.S.A. to Morocco.

Rommel's army was still struggling back up Halfaya Pass when, on the night of November 7-8, 1942, the expedition reached its appointed ports. There were three separate attacks. The first one, purely American, was

AFRICAN BEACH HEAD. *American troops haul guns and equipment ashore after slight opposition has been overcome.*

187

designed to land at Casablanca, on the Atlantic seaboard of Morocco. The second and third, mainly British in composition, appeared off Oran and Algiers simultaneously.

At all three ports the operations met with resistance. The destroyer *Broke* smashed in the boom at Algiers and was sunk in the harbour. The cutters *Walney* and *Hartland* fought their way to the quays at Oran, and riddled with shot, sank there, but troops carried in transports got ashore. In the main, French resistance was not determined, and within 48 hours the position of Allied occupation was generally accepted. At Casablanca, however, the Americans had to fight a full-scale naval battle and to sink most of the resisting French squadron, besides fighting their way ashore at the expense of 2,000 casualties, before firing at last ceased.

French Co-operation

Happily the political repercussions took a favourable turn. Immediately on learning the news, Hitler invaded Vichy France; and Admiral Darlan, who was in Algiers, declared in favour of the Allies, although his action was disavowed by Marshal Pétain and the Government at Vichy. Darlan, who was soon afterwards assassinated, appointed General Giraud as Commander of the French armed forces and instructed him to co-operate with General Eisenhower.

The forces which were landed lost no time in beginning their move towards Tunisia, for it was vital to make the most of the surprise sustained by the Germans and to seize strategic points before Rommel received reinforcements from the Italian mainland. In accordance with this, General Anderson and the First Army made a gallant attempt to seize Tunis itself.

By a narrow margin they were too late, for the Germans, moving with incredible alacrity, had got there first by transporting large numbers of troops and light weapons by air.

The First Army were forced to withdraw and the enemy at once began to build up a powerful and well equipped army and to occupy the mountains around both cities. For months the efforts of the Allied armies to force them back in rainy weather and mud proved unsuccessful

Final Break-through

All this time the Eighth Army had been driving on and its appearance within striking distance to the southeast closed the ring. Rommel's troops were driven back for one last stand in the Cape Bon peninsula. The secret transference of a large part of General Montgomery's war - hardened and experienced troops to the First Army contributed to the final break-through. The combined Allied air forces did splendid work.

When the time was judged ripe for the final, all-out assault, Tunis and Bizerta fell within a few hours of one another; and the Germans, who could not escape in any large numbers by sea or air, surrendered wholesale during the concluding stages of the operation, in its way a classic of military strategy. Rommel, his dreams of capturing Egypt now completely hopeless, had been withdrawn. His successor in the command, von Arnim, was captured along with all his staff. In all 300,000 men laid down their arms. One thousand guns and 250 tanks—with many supply dumps still undestroyed so swiftly had events moved—fell to the victors. The date was May 13, 1943 almost three years after the evacuation of Dunkirk. The wheel had indeed turned a full circle.

VICTORY PARADE. *Pipers of the 51st Highland Division lead the march through the streets of Tunis. The salute was taken by Generals Giraud, Anderson and Eisenhower.*

OCCUPATION COMPLETED. *Singing Nazi war songs as they march, German troop enter the great French Mediterranean seaport of Marseilles. The terms of the Armistic have been broken by the Germans as the Allied forces land in French North Afric From now until liberation, no part of France will be free from German exploitation*

GERMANS IN MARSEILLES

WHEN the terms of the Armistice were accepted by the French delegates in the Forest of Compiègne, a line was drawn across the map of France and the southern part left unoccupied. At Vichy was established the government of Marshal Pétain, nominally free, but in reality at the mercy of German influence.

The tide of battle had swept across the north, but the south had seen little actual fighting, and for a time the people of Unoccupied France made the best of things. Moreover, many of their men were prisoners of war, a fact which the Germans used as a shrewd, blackmailing threat to extort collaboration for Hitler's New Order.

Darlan and De Gaulle Broadcast

Then came the news of the Allied landings in North Africa and the appeals by Admiral Darlan, for long Marshal Pétain's right-hand man, and by General de Gaulle for all good Frenchmen to support the Allied action. The alarm bells rang in Berlin and were echoed in Vichy. A shock of reality swept through Unoccupied France. The Allies were well on their way to possess vital ports on the other side of the Mediterranean. Would the next move be an invasion of Europe via the South of France? On November 11, 1942, Hitler decided to extend his hold over France.

On the twenty-fourth anniversary of the armistice of World War No. 1, German armoured columns and infantry divisions crossed the demarcation line. They had orders from Hitler to cross France by the most direct route. Announcing this at six a.m., the German Consul-General in Vichy, Baron von Nidda, asked the French military and police to render all possible assistance to the German forces. He presented Pétain with a lengthy letter from Hitler stating that information suggested that the next objective of the Anglo-American forces would be Corsica and the South of France. "In consequence of this," he added, "the foundations of the Armistice have ceased to exist." Pétain solemnly protested against the violation of the armistice terms, but his protest was brushed contemptuously aside.

German Treachery

The German authorities consented to make one exception in the occupation. Following a promise by the naval chief at Toulon that they would defend themselves against any aggressor, it was agreed not to occupy this fortified area. This pact was broken.

Crossing the border, the Germans raced southwards. By ten a.m. a force was known to have reached Lyons and another Limoges, both approximately equidistant from Vichy, and the latter on the road which runs through Toulouse to become one of the main routes across the Pyrenees to Spain.

Speed was the watchword of the Germans. Commanders, driving at the heads of their columns, were afterwards reported to have spurred their men on again and again, declaring that it was of the highest importance that they should reach the coast as soon as possible. Meanwhile Italian forces fulfilled the old Fascist ambition —now somewhat staled by long waiting —to occupy Nice, Corsica and Savoy. In Marseilles and other Mediterranean towns the French with empty hearts and sullen faces watched the German convoys arrive. All France was in chains.

FRENCH SACRIFICE THEIR FLEET. *Disregarding their promise not to occupy Toulon, German armoured columns entered the port at 4 a.m. on November 27, 1942. Meanwhile the Luftwaffe mined the entrance to the harbour to prevent the great French Fleet from taking to the open sea, while the tanks and infantry entered the arsenal.*

For a moment Allied sea supremacy hung in the balance. Then blinding flashes lit the night sky as French seamen scuttled their ships. The Germans were held off, as ship after ship heeled over and sank to the bottom of the harbour. As is seen in the above photograph, dawn showed a scene of devastation. France had redeemed her pledge.

STALINGRAD'S GREAT STORY

BOMBED and unbelievably blasted by high explosive, Stalingrad—the name means "City of Steel" —came to be regarded as a symbol of resistance. For month after month the battle raged and vast areas of the city were reduced to ruin before the Russians snatched victory out of destruction and dealt a fearsome blow to the German Army. Never before had any city been subjected to a more ferocious, concentrated attack by land and air. Divisions of men were decimated as the full fury of armoured warfare was unleashed — tanks, armoured cars, artillery and automatic weapons of all kinds, high explosive, incendiary and oil bombs. Some of the fiercest fighting was done in the streets and shattered houses, with rifles, bayonets, hand grenades and dynamite. As casualties piled up to an enormous figure on both sides the world recalled the name by which Stalingrad (then Tsaritsyn) was called in the Civil War—the Red Verdun.

Pride of the Soviets

Where the River Don swings furthest to the east on its southward course it nears a western bend of the mighty River Volga. On the Volga's west bank at that point stands the vast manufacturing city of Stalingrad, greatest of all symbols of the Soviet Union's industrial achievements. It possessed great factories and finely planned streets. Its capture in the German summer campaign of 1942 would have been of tremendous strategic value in their bid to outflank Moscow from the east, cutting the great water-highway from the Caspian to the capital.

Hitler vowed that Stalingrad should be his. In mid-August von Bock, one of Germany's best generals, struck east across the Don, bringing to bear massed forces supported by the full weight of the Luftwaffe. Slowly the Germans progressed, until by all the "laws of war" the Russians might have been expected to abandon the city.

Every House a Fortress

It became apparent that Stalingrad would be defended to the last. On September 12 the Germans had reached the Volga north and south of the city, enclosing it in a semi-circle of fire. On the following day the defenders issued their battle-cry: "Death rather than surrender. The Red Army swears to hold Stalingrad and to defend the Fatherland to the death." Hundreds of Nazi planes were dive-bombing the town and heavy artillery kept up an unceasing bombardment. But the Russians remained in the city and prepared to repel each and every attack. Orders were given that each house must become a fortress, with water, food, ammunition and connecting tunnels. Most of the women, children and aged were evacuated, but of those who stayed young girls became telephonists in the underground staff headquarters or made hand grenades, and old peasant men and women manned boats on the Volga which kept open the supply lines.

German attacks swept into the city, preceded by swarms of tanks and stunning artillery fire. Each time the defenders sallied forth from cellars and dugouts and met their assailants with bullets, cold steel, and bombs. On September 30 Hitler announced that Stalingrad would certainly be taken. And early in October a German thrust penetrated almost to the Volga bank.

AT CLOSE QUARTERS. *Leaping through holes blasted in the walls, Red Army men drive the Germans from a Stalingrad building during the bitter house-to-house fighting.*

195

ASSAULT GROUP. *A Red Army lieutenant (extreme left) directs his men as they cover this Stalingrad building with withering fire before going in with bayonets.*

Under cover of the ruins were Russian snipers, machine-gunners, anti-tank gunners and grenadiers. Furniture was dragged out of houses and with smashed equipment from factories utilized for barriers across the streets.

Street fighting came to a stop only when buildings were being stormed. Houses were sometimes occupied partly by Germans and partly by Russians. As one side entered the ground floor they were sniped at from the floor above. Fierce hand-to-hand encounters raged on rickety stairways, machine guns stuttered forth from kitchen windows. During one day alone the Germans were hurled back from the centre of the city on 12 occasions and 42 of their tanks were smashed. "The ground has to be won yard by yard," admitted German commentators ruefully as division after division of crack troops were fed into this seemingly inexhaustible furnace. The world heard that the great Red Barricade gun factory had fallen together with much of the factory area.

Then, on November 22, it was announced that the Red Army had launched a powerful offensive from the north-west of the city *behind* the German Army, advancing across the Don bend from Voronezh. Both railway lines supplying the enemy on the east bank of the Don had been cut and the important supply base of Kalach captured.

Hitler's Rash Promise

Doubtless the German General Staff, had it been left to them, would have recognized the omens and withdrawn whilst there was still time. But Hitler had promised his people Stalingrad and would not willingly "lose face." So the Germans continued their abortive efforts while the trap closed.

Thrusting up from the south, cutting communications and lines of retreat, the Red Army pushed on until the trap was complete. It had been summer when the attack was launched, now it was the Russian winter.

Shivering in their dug-outs, with meagre supplies of food and ammunition flown to them, the Germans were told that a relief army was on its way. They were not told that the attempt had been made and had failed. So they continued to live on the carcasses of dead horses, with their bread supply cut to 5 ozs. a day, dying from hunger, exhaustion, disease, and the attacks launched against them in ever-increasing strength. The end came slowly and miserably. Some 195,000 were still alive on January 8, 1943, when Marshal Timoshenko called upon them to surrender. They refused. The Fuehrer had ordered them to fight.

And then, on January 31, the miserable remnants of the once proud force gave in. Field Marshal von Paulus and 15 generals, some of them bitter with anger at the strategy which had thrown away so many men, were among those who were captured. By February 2, 91,000 troops in all, including 34 generals and 2,500 officers, were in Russian hands. Of the 6th Army only 12,000 remained, and many of those were ill or wounded.

Germany Mourns

Some of the captured generals were reported to have said that the flower of their army, the toughest, fittest, and most seasoned men, had perished in what had been the greatest single military disaster in history. Its extent may be judged by the fact that 330,000 men had been trapped originally.

The Russians lost no time in starting to repair the city and in improvising hospital services, water supplies, and electricity. Column after column of woeful German prisoners were marched away. And in Germany two days of mourning was decreed.

CAMOUFLAGE. *Reserve troops pass through a village on their way to Stalingrad. White covering merges into the snow-covered steppes, for the Russian winter has come.*

RELIEF OF LENINGRAD. *Breaking of the German ring round Russia's " window into the West " enabled food and ammunition to pour into this besieged Baltic port.*

Smiling citizens watch long columns of shaven-headed prisoners escorted through the streets of their city. The vital lifeline between Russia and her Allies is now freed.

FINAL PUSH ON GUADALCANAL. *Stripped to the waist beneath the sweltering tropic heat, these American gunners blast away with a 155 mm. cannon at the Japanese defences during the final stages of the Guadalcanal offensive in the January of 1943.*

Japanese snipers lashed to branches of trees, raiding parties that crept forward under the cover of darkness, made the advance through the swamps and tangled undergrowth a slow, costly process. It was sheer determination that enabled the Americans to hold out.

GUADALCANAL TRIUMPH

IN the Japanese plan the highest importance was attached to possession of the Solomon Islands, the value of which as an advanced base may be gauged from a glance at the map on pages 160 and 161. Construction of airfields and supply dumps was interrupted by an American landing in the August of 1942, and between then and February, 1943, the Japanese made costly and determined attempts to regain complete control of the island of Guadalcanal, upon which for some time the U.S. forces were able to maintain only a precarious foothold.

Enemy Night Landings

The enemy built up their forces by skilful night landings on Guadalcanal. By September they were ready to launch a full-scale attack, which was heroically repelled by the outnumbered American garrison. From then onward great battles were fought as time after time the enemy sought to land sufficient reinforcements to drive the Allied troops into the sea. Not once, but many times the fate of the entire operation depended upon those engagements; once the Allied supply line was cut the whole position would have speedily become hopeless.

" I suppose there is no spot in the world where there has been so much fighting in such a small area as Guadalcanal—at sea and in the air and on land," said an American Marine officer who had fought there. " For three months we held about 15 square miles and even when there were not major attacks against the perimeter of the airfield, there were daily patrol clashes. Five major naval engagements were fought off the shores of Guadalcanal from August to November, en-

tirely at night. During the first few months there were almost daily aerial fights."

When darkness fell with tropic suddenness the Marines guarding the airfield had to be at the highest pitch of efficiency, with eyes like cats' to pierce the blackness and ears trained to detect the slightest sound that might betoken a Japanese raid. The cracking of a twig or the rustle of leaves might be the only warning of the enemy's presence, moving in small groups fanwise across the jungle.

Malaria, dysentery and incredible discomfort from insects plagued the American forces, although emergency hospital services were quickly and efficiently improvised. But at the beginning of the long fight all supplies were short.

Particularly were the odds against the American airmen heavy, the ratio at one time being one American aircraft to ten available to the enemy. On one occasion there was only one serviceable dive bomber to attack a large Japanese convoy of supplies.

Gradually the technical resources and the quality of their fighting men enabled the Americans to go over to the offensive, to the accompaniment of tremendous damage to enemy shipping and Japanese bases on Rabaul and other islands.

Slowly Guadalcanal was mopped up in spite of fanatical resistance. Fortified positions in enemy hands had to be blown to pieces during the progress by the Americans across the mountainous, intensely difficult terrain of the island.

Not until February 10, 1943, six months after the first landing, could it be announced that Guadalcanal was completely cleared.

ISLAND HOPPING. *After consolidating their hold on the southern Solomons, the Americans landed on Bougainville, to the north of the group, on November 1, 1943. In the above photograph combat troops are seen swarming aboard landing craft. American Coastguardsmen were among those manning the barges in this further invasion.*

BATTLE OF THE SICILIAN NARROWS. *Twenty-five out of a formation of thirty-five J.U.52 transport planes were shot out of the air when B.25 Mitchells and P.38 Lightnings of the North-West African Air Force swooped down over the Sicilian Narrows. The Germans were trying desperately hard to reinforce their Sicilian garrison.*

This remarkable photograph shows the Mitchells turning away after the first deadly attack. Cannon shells whip up the placid Mediterranean waters beneath the enemy aircraft which are to be seen flying in ragged formation near the sea. Thus it was that the way was paved for the Allied beach-heads on Sicily, the next step nearer to Italy.

CAMPAIGN IN SICILY

THE Allied plan for the invasion of the Continent of Europe was wide and comprehensive. Italy was scheduled as the first European country upon which Allied soldiers would land; in preparation the approaches to the southern end of the Axis had to be cleaned up and a clear way made across the Mediterranean for the powerful forces that had been prepared in readiness.

Airborne Attack Begins

The small island of Pantelleria, situated off Cape Bon (the scene of the final German defeat in Africa), surrendered to British troops on June 11 after day and night bombardments from the sea and from the air. The small island had long been the base for enemy mine-laying operations and its control was essential to future operations. This left three more or less strongly defended islands on the route to Italy. These were Sicily, Sardinia and Corsica, and of these Sicily was by far the strongest and the pivot of the approach to the mainland. The island possessed 50 or so airfields which would be a vast asset to the Allied air arm, and an essential factor in the invasion of Italy.

The attack began by British and American air-borne troops on July 10, after a preliminary softening-up campaign from the air, during which numbers of enemy fighters were destroyed and heavy damage done. At ten o'clock at night gliders, followed by paratroops, dropped behind the enemy's lines in Sicily. It was the first

NAVAL COVER. *Enemy shore batteries score a hit on an Allied warship during the Sicilian invasion. Six ships were lost.*

large-scale landing by sea attempted by the Allies and mistakes were made, but these were rectified by superb fighting qualities and rapid thinking in emergencies. The air-borne troops had the task of capturing selected points and attacking coastal defences from the rear. Some of them fell in the perilous moment of landing, but the rest went about their work grimly and efficiently under the cover of darkness.

For the main forces, to be transported by sea, Admiral of the Fleet, Sir Andrew Cunningham, was responsible for 3,266 surface craft, comprising ships of every size and purpose, from battleships to fast-moving M.T.B.s. Before this great armada embarked, the admiral had given them the following message : " Our primary duty is to place this vast expedition ashore in the minimum time and subsequently to maintain our military and air forces as they drive relentlessly forward into enemy territory. In the light of this duty great risks must and are to be accepted."

Zero Hour Scene

Zero hour was 3 a.m. on the morning of the 10th ; troops swarmed ashore from the landing craft at many points. Some were easy, but at others the invaders dashed up the beaches to destroy the pillbox defences and silence the crashing gun batteries that opposed them. It was a scene to be repeated afterwards in Italy and France, but the determination of the Allied troops and their coolness under fire were not to be surpassed. By 7 a.m. landings had been established along 70 miles of coastline and infantry were pressing into the interior. The valuable harbour of Pescara had been taken, and next day

Canadians drove into an airfield. Thenceforward the invasion proceeded with amazing precision. The enemy had been surprised, not by the invasion, but by the points selected for the initial landings. The German-Italian forces were driven steadily back, as the Americans drove westwards along the coast, taking Agrigento and advancing to Palermo ; the Canadians took Ragusa and drove a broadening ridge into the heart of the island. To the Eighth Army fell the task of driving along from Syracuse and Augusta to the plain of Catania. This port itself faced the toe of Italy, and was clearly the vital test of strength.

By great efforts the enemy held the Eighth, but the Americans and the Canadians, steadily forging ahead, came down from the north coast in an irresistible tide and caught the German rear. With the smashing of the resistance at Catania the campaign was virtually at an end as far as full-scale operations were concerned.

By the time Catania had fallen it must have been apparent to the Germans that they could only gain time—time to get their remaining men off the island and to prepare for the Italian invasion which cast its shadow before. The Eighth were already pressing forward towards Messina, the port on the tip of the island facing the mainland. The enemy sowed mines in profusion. The terrain itself was not smooth by any means and captured German mules proved invaluable in the mountainous regions. Then, on August 10, the Eighth Army linked up with the American Seventh, and on the 17th of the month the Americans were announced to have taken Messina.

LANDING BEGINS. *British infantry wade through the water as the landing craft discharge their cargoes on to the beaches.*

MOPPING UP. *The Eighth Army has entered Catania, principal port of Sicily, and some of them are seen here engaged in mopping up among the ruins of a convent, taken over by the enemy as a strong point. These operations provided a foretaste of the grim battles ahead during the invasions of Italy and France; every yard was contested.*

For the Italians, the fall of Sicily marked the beginning of the end. Allied troops were enthusiastically welcomed by the local inhabitants, but they were to encounter systematic destruction by the Germans of everything that would be of slightest value to the Allies. Power stations and other public works were blown up, and houses mined.

NEW GUINEA OFFENSIVE

SEPTEMBER 4, 1943, saw the Australian Army launch an all-out offensive in New Guinea (also known as Papua). Since the summer of 1942 the Australians had been fighting against a well-supplied and ruthless enemy in this large island, separated from the Australian mainland at its nearest point by the Torres Strait. They had been exposed to some of the worst climatic conditions possible for white men; they had on many occasions lacked essential equipment; but although outnumbered they had never been outfought.

Drive Through the Mountains

The early attempts by the enemy to seize the vital regions of Milne Bay and Port Morcsby were beaten off. Not only this, but the Australians went over to the offensive, driving the enemy back over the Owen Stanley Mountains, and, in collaboration with the Americans, captured Gona, Sanananda and Buna after desperate fighting. Lessons concerning supply were learned and applied, air transport facilitating the movement of men and material over country in which the only possible alternative was heartbreaking marching and the manhandling of every piece of equipment. During the battle for Buna, for instance, jeeps and 25-pounders were landed from the air.

In the January-February of 1943, the Japanese retaliated by an attack on Wau, with the intention of using it as an air base against Fort Moresby and a bastion against further Allied attacks. In the early days defence of this region had been left to the New Guinea Volunteer Rifles, composed of men, principally civilians, who knew the country well. They had not sufficient strength to risk pitched battles, but as skirmishers and "commandos" they operated with outstanding success. They took the first shock of the new Japanese threat before reinforcements were rushed up by air.

Sea and Air Landings

By February Wau, with its small airfield, was safe. Then began a campaign to drive the enemy back, and capture the coastal port of Salamanaua. Every mile was fanatically defended, but the Australian machine ground its way forward, crushing thousands of crack Japanese troops, until, by September 3, the fall of the port was certain.

Then began the spectacular stage of Australian-American operations. Supported by the American Navy and Air Force, the Australian 9th Division landed on the shores of the Huon Gulf and drove towards Lae. Simultaneously, the 7th Division, taken by air to Nadzab, advanced on the port from inland. The town fell and the surviving enemy took to the hills in a frantic effort to escape.

No rest was granted to the Japanese. On the night of September 22, the 9th made another landing from the sea, storming heavily fortified beaches to capture Finschafen on October 2. For the first time tanks—British Matildas—were used.

By a triumph of planning, pressure was maintained north towards Sio. Meanwhile American units based at Finschafen, by-passed the coast along which the Australians were struggling, and landed from the sea at Saidor. There they waited until the Australians, having taken Sio Mission on January 14, 1944, lined up with their brothers-in-arms on February 10.

JUNGLE DRAMA. *The camera records a tense moment in the Australian advance in New Guinea. A Japanese detachment has been driven back, leaving their dead and equipment. Australians find nothing but Japanese corpses and the evidence of flight.*

213

DICTATOR'S END

B Y July, 1943, the accumulated disgraces arising from her cynical entry into the war had brought Italy to disaster. She had lost her African territories, in Sicily only one corner remained, and that was held by the Germans. "Mare nostrum"— our sea, as Mussolini termed the Mediterranean—had been turned into a British lake. There remained inadequate weapons, dispirited troops, and war-weary civilians in the face of the impending invasion of the Italian mainland.

At this crisis, Benito Mussolini, who had once scoffed at the idea of democracy under arms, went cap in hand to Hitler to ask for help. He got cold comfort from his fellow dictator, who was reported to have demanded in turn more concessions from Italy.

Five days later, on July 23, the Fascist Grand Council met for the first time since 1939. Mussolini made his confession of bankruptcy. The President, Grandi, strongly criticised the white-faced "leader," demanding that the King should be allowed to take over the reins. Ciano, Mussolini's son-in-law, railed bitterly at the Duce, the man to whom he personally owed everything. The wrangle lasted 19 hours, at the end of which Mussolini was defeated.

Next morning the erstwhile leader was put under protective arrest, Marshal Badoglio taking command. The structure that had looked so imposing for 21 years, the example that had inspired Hitler, was finally smashed and a military dictatorship took its place.

The Duce himself was rescued from his mountain prison by Nazi parachute troops. He was taken by 'plane to Hitler's H.Q., thenceforth to live as a

MUSSOLINI AND MASTER. *The fallen Duce with Hitler ' somewhere in Germany.'*

puppet dancing to the strings pulled by the man he had once professed to despise as an upstart.

Besides Mussolini, other fanatical Fascists succeeded in escaping to German-held territory. Under the nominal guidance of the Duce, who was reported to be seriously ill, they

The Italian dictator was saved from falling into Allied hands by Nazi paratroops. His splendid uniforms were left behind; henceforth he is to exist as Hitler's pensioner.

formed a "Republican Fascist Party," and attributed the fall of Italy to the machinations of the Italian Royal House and King Victor Emmanuel.

Mussolini's son-in-law, Count Ciano, the man who had handed the declaration of war to the French and British ambassadors, fell into German hands whilst endeavouring to escape. After a nominal trial he was executed as a traitor—an object lesson to other politicians who might be considering escape from the Axis camp.

In southern Italy, meanwhile, democratic institutions and free speech were steadily restored to the people.

BLASTING JAPANESE SHIPPING. *On November 2, 1943, medium bombers attached to the Fifth U.S. Army Air Force struck at the shipping off the great Japanese base of Rabaul. This photograph indicates the extent of the damage, which prevented enemy reinforcements reaching Bougainville. Fifteen Japanese ships were destroyed.*

As the result of General MacArthur's strategy the Japanese garrison on Rabaul, estimated to be about 22,000 strong, became isolated. This process of by-passing large groupings of enemy troops, cutting off their supplies by persistent naval and air offensives, was an essential part of the Allied plan of attack on Japan's forces.

A FLEET SUBMITS

IT is September 10, 1943; the scene is the Maltese port of Valetta. Against a background of white buildings, sun-lit quays, bomb-scarred ruins, thousands of people gaze across the deep blue sea. It is no ordinary occasion, for on this day the ordeal of the island fortress is ended : part of the Italian Fleet is coming in to surrender.

Although one's mind goes back to the German surrender at Scapa Flow in November, 1918, the circumstances are far different, since the Italians are allowed to keep their ships, guns and ammunition, subject to Allied control. Except for a few instances of fine self-sacrifice the fleet has not covered itself with glory; nevertheless it comprises many powerful, fast, modern weapons. "Its acquisition alone would have justified the armistice," is General Eisenhower's verdict.

So, on this sunny morning, a double line of warships, newly painted grey, slowly steamed into the magnificent Grand Harbour; they were escorted by dazzle-painted ships of the British Navy—the giants *Warspite* and *Valiant*, with their tremendous superstructures, besides a brave show of cruisers and destroyers. From one of the latter Sir Andrew Cunningham and General Eisenhower witnessed the scene.

The Italians wore ceremonial dress—red jackets, blue trousers and white hats. The surrender involved 108 ships of all kinds, 28 of which went to Malta. They included the battleships *Littorio* and *Vittorio Veneto*, the modernized older battleships *Caio Duilio* and *Andrea Doria*, 6 cruisers and 7 destroyers.

MALTA LOOKS ON. *Outside the Harbour of Valetta, the backbone of the Italian Navy is lined up for its formal surrender.*

NORTH-WEST OF SALERNO. *British troops are seen taking cover in the ruins of a half-demolished house as they near the small town of Cava, north-west of Salerno.*

ALLIES STRIKE AGAIN

THE invasion of Italy, which was unexpectedly easy at first, came somewhat as an anti-climax. After the fierce resistance the Germans had put up in Sicily, it was expected that the mainland opposition, aided by high mountains, narrow coastal roads, and other natural obstacles backed by powerful artillery, would prove a tough nut even for the battle-hardened veterans of the Eighth Army to crack.

But the shell of the nut had been cracked by a fortnight's pitiless bombing. Almost every place from Reggio to Naples, and certainly every rail junction worth noticing, had been plastered time after time with bombs. Also, on the afternoon of August 31, 1943, the battleships *Rodney* and *Nelson*, with a cruiser and nine destroyers, had sailed into the Straits of Messina and had pounded the enemy batteries with their 16 in. guns.

Italian Armistice

This bombardment may have confirmed the Germans in their intention of retreating to the north, where they could obtain more elbow room. In addition Italy had suffered a mortal blow by the loss of her Sixth Army, 300,000 strong, in Sicily. Mussolini had fallen and his successor in power, Marshal Badoglio, had made overtures to the Allies for an armistice. This was granted on September 3, although it was not publicly announced until four days later. Thus, when at 4.30 in the morning of September 3, vast numbers of landing craft and small ships laden with troops made their appearance in the Straits, under the cover of an enormous air umbrella, they met comparatively little opposition. Landings were effected all along

the shore between Reggio and San Giovanni; by nightfall the Canadians had seized Reggio aerodrome and the first Allied landing on the mainland of Hitler's Europe had been made.

Italian soldiers of all ranks surrendered wholesale without even token resistance. On the 8th another landing, this time at Taranto, gave the invaders a base behind the Italian "toe."

The first stage of the invasion had been successfully accomplished, though powerful German forces had yet to be met and smashed in battle.

Near Disaster at Salerno

While the Eighth were progressing against little opposition, a bloody struggle took place on the beaches of Salerno, which came desperately close to being an Allied disaster. The High Command had decided upon an assault in the midst of the German lines by throwing almost an entire army ashore at Salerno, a few miles south of Naples. It was almost at the limit of the range of Allied shore-based aircraft, and from the beginning the Germans, who soon assembled three panzer and several infantry divisions, hit back fiercely.

The Allied air force made superhuman efforts, making over 2,000 sorties in a single day, but at one time the German tanks drove the British and Americans to within three miles of the sea. Then the Eighth Army succeeded in linking up with the Americans as it drove up from the south, and by the 17th the Germans reluctantly began to withdraw to Naples. It had been a near thing. "From the 3rd to the 7th day," said Mr. Churchill afterwards, "the possibility of a large-scale disaster could not be excluded."

SALERNO BEACH. *As the enemy steadily retreat from the coastal areas men of the Allied 5th Army are pouring supplies of all sorts ashore at the Salerno Bay beaches.*

This landing took place on September 9, as the 8th Army captured Taranto. Forces engaged in the operation consisted of an equal number of British and Americans.

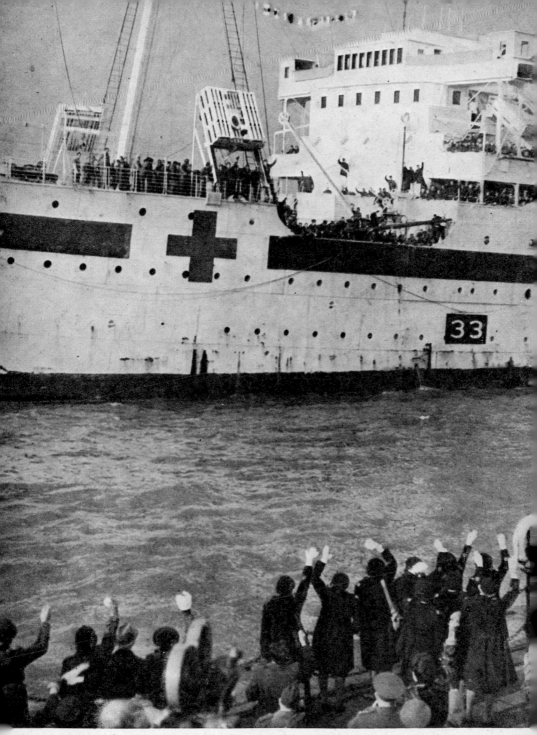

THEY'RE HOME AGAIN. *As the liner* Atlantis *with repatriated prisoners on deck, nears a British port their wives and families are at the dock to wave a welcome to them.*

DRAMA OF REPATRIATION

THERE is a stir on the quayside. A great liner is coming into port, her side distinguished by an enormous painted red cross. Excited men, some on crutches, some leaning on the rails, wave down at people ashore; others turn their heads from the stretchers on which they have been placed, seeking a glimpse of home; some, with sightless eyes, sense the smell of land with their nostrils and say, "There it is." A reception committee waits by the gangplank, Red Cross nurses smile, another batch of repatriated British prisoners of war have arrived back home.

This was the scene enacted many times during the course of the war, but one the poignancy of which never failed to strike at the hearts of those who witnessed it. The work of effecting these exchanges was a part of the merciful duties performed so well by the International Red Cross.

The first exchange was made with the Italians, 60 badly wounded Britishers landing in Britain from *Llandovery Castle* on April 7, 1942. The Germans proved less accommodating to deal with, but after negotiations had broken down more than once an agreement was reached which ensured a steady flow of servicemen, medical personnel and interned British citizens back to their native land. Procedure involved the arrival in neutral countries of the German and Allied subjects concerned and their exchange under Red Cross supervision.

Those who returned included men who had spent five years in a prison hospital or behind barbed wire. Most of them suffered from physical disabilities, and for these all that British medical science could perform, all that patience and encouragement in rehabilitation processes could accomplish, was not too good. As General Sir Robert F. Adam, Adjutant General to the Forces, said : "I only want to say how proud we have all been of the way you have borne yourselves as prisoners of war and how glad we are to see you back at last."

Many hundreds of families rejoiced at the return of some loved one: whole streets were decked with welcoming notices at the news that "one of the boys was on his way home." Such scenes of heartfelt gratitude were rehearsals of the great, national rejoicings which were to take place when the collapse of Germany took place, and all the men in the German prison camps were able to see their homes again.

FATHER AND SON. *A British corporal, repatriated home, hugs his small son who has met him at a London railway station.*

U.S. MARINES ON TARAWA. *On November 20, 1943, U.S. Marines, under Rear-Admiral Harry W. Hill and Major-General Julian C. Smith, landed on the important Japanese air base of Tarawa in the Gilbert Islands. Terrific enemy fire met them as they stormed their way up the beaches, taking cover behind the flimsy palm trees as they went.*

This photograph shows the Marines going in to attack in one of the bloodiest battles in
their stirring history. The Japanese garrison, protected by 500 strongly defended pill
boxes, fought almost to the last man. The Americans lost 1,025 killed and 2,257
wounded, while the total cost to the enemy was estimated as in the region of 5,000.

EAST MEETS WEST

ON December 2, 1943, the news was broken to the world that President Roosevelt, Mr. Winston Churchill, and Marshal Chiang Kai-shek had met in a vitally important conference, beginning on November 21 and ending on the 26th. The meeting place was described as "Somewhere in North Africa," which concealed the actual venue—the Mena House Hotel, a short distance outside Cairo.

This was the first meeting between the three leaders, and its object was to reach a working understanding regarding the many major issues arising from the war against Japan. As a country which had been at war for twelve years, with many of her richest and most fertile regions under Japanese domination, China was in a parlous economic position, lacking weapons and supplies of all sorts. This had become increasingly serious since the closing of the Burma road.

The military delegates, representing the highest authority on fighting at sea, on land and in the air, threshed out many pressing problems, while the diplomatic representatives performed an equally urgent task.

It was, of course, impossible to issue any statement on military matters, for the plans made could only be judged by the successes gained in the Pacific during the following year, but a declaration was made outlining specific war aims. It was foreshadowed that Manchuria and the Island of Formosa, both seized by Japan, would be returned to China; while Korea, then a Japanese slave-state, would be granted independent existence. Further, it was announced that Japan would be deprived of the numerous Pacific islands which she had acquired and fortified since the end of the First World War.

228

CAIRO CONFERENCE. *Outside the Mena House Hotel, Cairo, at the conclusion of the historic meeting between the leaders of Great Britain, China and the U.S.A.*

The photograph above shows :—front row (left to right), Marshal Chiang Kai-shek, President Roosevelt, Mr. Churchill, and Madame Chiang. Back row (left to right), General Chang Chen, Lt.-Gen. Ling Wai, Lt.-Gen. Somervell, Lt.-Gen. Stilwell, General Arnold, Field-Marshal Sir John Dill, Admiral Lord Louis Mountbatten.

SWORD OF HONOUR. *Mr. Churchill has handed the Stalingrad Sword to Marshal Stalin.*
Their handshake symbolises the friendship reached between Britain and the U.S.S.R.

HISTORY IN THE MAKING

NOT the least important reason for the successful handling of the war by the Big Three—Britain, America and Russia—was the periodic conferences between the three Prime Ministers.

The consultations at Teheran occurred at a time (November 28 to December 1, 1943) when the Germans still occupied much of Russia and the invasion of Italy was still recent history. The main aim was to arrange for co-ordinated action against the common foe. The conference also yielded hopes of post-war co-operation, which led directly to the Dumbarton Oaks plan for a renewed and vigorous international association of nations in time of peace. "We came here," said a joint statement after the deliberations were over, "with hope and determination. We leave here friends, in fact, in spirit and in purpose."

Scene of the Discussions

Mr. Churchill and the President had travelled from Egypt with their advisers. Marshal Stalin, accompanied by M. Molotov and Marshal Voroshilov, had arrived at the Soviet Embassy in the Iranian capital the previous day, November 26. The British were lodged at the British Legation next door, President Roosevelt accepting Stalin's offer of hospitality. There, amid the flower-beds of the beautiful grounds, with snow-capped mountains for a background, conversations continued for three days between the leaders, while the military advisers discussed plans in constant session.

It was arranged that Germany should be attacked simultaneously from Poland, from Normandy, and from the Mediterranean. Just one year after

Stalin aptly summed up the results by saying, "There are few instances in history of plans for large-scale military operations undertaken jointly against a common enemy being carried out so fully and with such precision." Concerning post-war problems, the official statement included the significant phrase, " With our diplomatic advisers we have surveyed the problems of the future."

When next the statesmen representing the three powers were to meet, armies would be hammering at Germany itself from the east and from the west. The consultations at Teheran may truly be said to have sounded the death-knell of Hitler's German empire and its leaders.

Tribute to Stalingrad

An impressive event at Teheran was the presentation of the Stalingrad Sword of Honour. Early in the year, on the anniversary of the formation of the Red Army, King George VI announced that he had ordered the sword to be made, for presentation to the people of Stalingrad in token of the admiration in which Great Britain held them. The sword, a beautiful piece of British craftsmanship made of Sheffield steel, was presented by Mr. Churchill to Stalin within the Soviet Embassy, with British and Russian Guards of Honour lining the walls. The blade bore the inscription, "To the steel-hearted citizens of Stalingrad, the gift of King George VI, in token of the homage of the British people." Stalin, who was visibly moved by the tribute, kissed the blade and handed the sword to Marshal Voroshilov: after inspection it was given into the custody of the Russian guard of Honour.

ANZIO LANDING

At two o'clock in the morning of January 22, 1944, General Alexander, whose reputation for springing surprises had become proverbial, outwitted the German General Kesselring by a totally unexpected landing far in the enemy rear and only 30 miles from the City of Rome.

For all too long there had been a bitter struggle in the mud and the mountains from Minturno to Pescara, and especially on the Rapido and Garigliano Rivers. Determined to hold out at all costs, Kesselring had just ordered up from Rome three more panzer divisions when news reached him that the British and Americans had slipped ashore 60 miles to his rear.

The expedition was fully provided by air cover, operating from bases which enabled aircraft to stay up for a reasonable time. Warships supported the landing with their guns. "Ducks," amphibious transport vehicles that in themselves were a miracle of ingenuity, waddled ashore and carried their loads several miles inland.

R.A.F. bombers strafed enemy communications, and on the second day more troops, tanks and guns were landed at Nettuno, the place first seized, and at Anzio. Before them lay an open plain, with hills and the Appian Way to Rome 8 to 10 miles inland. Not until the heads of our armoured units approached the high ground did fighting commence on a large scale. Then Kesselring, already hard pressed on the original Italian front, rushed up his panzers in a furious and unsuccessful attack.

SOUTH OF ROME. *Allied troops watch two destroyers laying a smoke screen as the fleet moves in to anchor off Anzio beach.*

ORDEAL OF CASSINO

T HE fight for Cassino equalled in ferocity and exceeded in duration that at Stalingrad; it lasted more than five and a half months, during which Americans, British, Indians and French on the one hand, and Germans on the other, fought and died in thousands on the surrounding hills and within the crater-pitted and rubbish-strewn streets. The little ancient town lies right under the shadow of the steep Monte Cassino ("Monastery Hill"), which was crowned by the most famous of all Benedictine Abbeys. A small stream, the Rapido, had been diverted by the Germans so that the meadows were flooded. It was winter, snowy, misty, rainy, with the valleys deep in mud and the hills covered by treacherous drifts of snow.

The high road to Rome, having surmounted Mt. Trocchio (which the Fifth Army captured after a bitter fight on January 15) wound through Cassino and back round Monastery Hill to the railway station. Opposite the latter, across the river, lay the ancient Roman amphitheatre, the fire from which made a secure hold on the station impossible by the Allies.

Forcing the Gustav Line

The whole district formed part of the Gustav Line, an elaborate series of fortified hills, with cunningly hidden pillboxes, barbed wire tangles, booby traps, mines and ditches. It soon became evident, even when a crossing of the Rapido had been forced, that Cassino could not be taken at once by direct assault. Free French troops, therefore, worked round the hills to the north and obtained a certain amount of success. Then on February 3 Americans of the 34th division, comprising tanks

and infantry, fought their way along the main highway into the suburbs of the town. Once having got a foothold in the town, the Americans began systematically to penetrate into it bit by bit. But the Germans turned every house into a fortress.

Cassino bristled with German self-propelled guns. The hard-hitting Hermann Goering Brigade fought desperately and were supplemented by men of the 1st Parachute Division—picked, battle-hardened troops of the highest order. For a week the struggle went on, the Americans advancing inch by inch; to cross a street was suicide and the prison and the Hotel Continental (in which the enemy had planted a tank) held the advance completely.

The Germans were using the Abbey, half a mile away, as an ideal observation point; and for some weeks not an Allied shell or bomb was permitted on this historic building. On February 10 the Americans smashed the prison.

On the 15th it was decided to bomb the Abbey and wave after wave of planes showered missiles on the stout walls. Then guns took up the job, but still Germans remained in the ruins, helped by an elaborate tunnel system. On the 18th New Zealanders, advancing after a terrific barrage, made an all-out effort to capture the town, but the weather enabled the Germans to avoid total defeat. So matters lay through April and early May. Then General Alexander brought down from the north-east a large part of the Eighth Army. The enemy began to withdraw, and on the morning of May 18 a gallant Polish detachment rushed and occupied Monastery Hill, while the British mopped up the town

HILL OF DEATH. *A pall of smoke wreathes the slopes of Monastery Hill, scene of some of the bitterest fighting of the war. At the top perches the old Benedictine Abbey.*

SMASHING GERMAN INDUSTRY. *Despite heavy clouds these Liberators of the 8th American Air Force seek out an aircraft factory in Central Germany and drop their heavy bomb loads with unerring accuracy on this vital target. A master plan had been drawn up preparatory to the invasion of the Continent of Europe which aimed at the*

progressive destruction of German war industry. Thanks to increasingly efficient tech-nique this programme was carried out to schedule and German arms production slowed. The full effects of these damaging and persistent attacks from the air were not felt at once ; but the failure of the Luftwaffe after D-Day was one of the results achieved.

FIVE PRIME MINISTERS. *The camera records an informal chat before the London Conference began. Left to right appear Mr. Mackenzie King (Canada), Field-Marshal*

EMPIRE POLICY

Smuts (*South Africa*), *Mr. Churchill, Mr. Fraser* (*N.Z.*), *and Mr. Curtin* (*Australia*).

THE solidarity of the British Empire in 1939 and after had been a source of amazement to many people in other countries, who had not, perhaps, fully grasped the fact that the Dominions and the Mother country had developed an association of free states, linked together by common ideas, tradition and mutual respect, and at war with the Axis by reason of their own free choice.

In early May, 1944, a meeting took place in London of the five prime ministers of the British Empire—Mr. Churchill (Britain), Mr. Mackenzie King (Canada), Mr. John Curtin (Australia), Mr. Peter Fraser (New Zealand) and Field-Marshal Smuts (South Africa). In Mr. Churchill's words the conference ensured that "we will all go along together in the fullest war effort until peace and justice have been established on unshakeable foundations."

The London Conference, although its immediate results were military, envisaged the part to be played by the British Empire when the war was over. The spirit of this was expressed in the declaration of the Conference, which affirmed that: "Mutual respect and honest conduct between nations is our chief desire. We are determined to work with all peace-loving peoples in order that tyranny and aggression shall be removed or, if need be, struck down wherever it raises its head. The peoples of the British Empire and Commonwealth of Nations willingly make their sacrifice to the common cause.

"We seek no advantages for ourselves at the cost of others. We desire the welfare and social advance of all nations and that they may help each other to better and broader days."

THE ROAD TO ROME

W HEN Cassino fell General Alexander's men were faced with a mass of tangled rubble sown with booby traps and mines of every description. It was no part of Allied strategy to give the enemy time to reorganize, and lumbering bulldozers were called up immediately to clear paths through the stricken town. Meanwhile Kesselring, who was to become known as Germany's supreme defensive genius, prepared for the battle for the approaches to Rome.

Outflanking the Adolf Hitler Line

Eighth Army tanks, squelching through mud and slush, rumbled up to engage in terrific gun duels with the batteries manning the so-called Adolf Hitler Line across the Liri Valley. The prisoners who came in stated that instructions had been issued to "resist until the last breath." By May 22, 1944, the Fifth Army were moving steadily along the Appian Way, the great road to Rome. This drive, linking up with the Anzio forces, threatened to outflank the Adolf Hitler Line, which was itself showing cracks under heavy pressure.

By June 3, Velletri, keypoint along the Appian Way backed by the Alban Hills, was entered, its stone houses shattered by repeated shelling. It had been one of the objectives of the Anzio landing, and during the winter its defences had looked down mockingly on the Allied troops beneath. What was even more important, the other hinge of the Rome defences, the town of Valmontone, on Highway 6, was stormed by American tanks. The German communique stated that: "At daybreak the enemy laid down a drumfire barrage on the German lines, after

putting a smokescreen over his own positions. As the curtain of shellfire crept up the hillside the enemy tanks pushed forward with mounted infantry in four distinct waves."

Only seventeen miles to the southeast Canadians of the Eighth Army took Ferenento, paving the way for a link-up between the Eighth and the Fifth Armies, and trapping the thousands of Germans seeking to withdraw back towards Rome. British paratroops were dropped ahead of the Allied lines to aid Italian guerrillas to impede the enemy flight, and these instructions went forth over radio stations in liberated Italy: "The Nazis are in full retreat and a bottle-neck in the traffic may mean the destruction of hundreds of German motor vehicles and armoured cars. Even without using weapons it is possible to render effective help to the Allies by blocking roads and destroying bridges. For the necessary explosives the patriots must get in touch with their comrades working in arms factories . . ."

Entering the City

It was apparent that Kesselring could make no effective stand south of the Italian capital, and the fate of Rome became a matter of urgent speculation. As had been the case over Cassino Monastery, the Germans attempted to gain time by talking of the possible damage to the city if it were defended. They got nowhere by such appeals, and started to withdraw their men and machines without delay.

By this time the Germans were demolishing the bridges over the Tiber, and troops of the Fifth Army were approaching the limits of the city. Enemy rearguards, with the usual orders to fight to the last man, plastered

WELCOME. *As the Allies drive through the streets of Rome a priest from the historic Church of St. Peter speaks to General Mark Clark, leader of the American Fifth Army.*

tanks and lorries advancing along Highway 6, with the suburbs of Rome, enveloped in blue-grey summer mist, within sight of the liberating Americans.

Then, at 7.15 on the morning of June 4, American troops were engaging the remnants of the German rearguards on the outskirts of Rome. By the evening tanks were streaming in, and with them came Allied administrators to take over the first Axis capital to fall to the might of Allied arms. Though Italy's greatest city had fallen, the Germans showed that they intended to cling on to the industrial regions of the north, which barred the way into Austria.

STORY OF D-DAY

SHORTLY before midnight on June 5, 1944, the familiar drone of hundreds of aeroplane engines above the south coast of Britain caused people to lift the black-out curtains of their rooms and peer up at the sky. For months the noise of Allied bombers going out and returning had been heard, but that night it seemed to be much louder than before.

In the months past it had heralded the blasting of gun-sites, the destruction of airfield runways, the demolition of bridges, all over northern and western France. During May alone the Anglo-American Air Forces had unloaded more than 20,000 tons of bombs there, systematically destroying communications between the German coastal armies and their bases further inland. Fifty out of 82 main rail centres had been destroyed, and 25 more damaged; only three bridges over the River Seine remained available to bear traffic.

But by June 5 the signal for invasion had been given, The planes, 1,300 strong, were going to blast ten coastal batteries between Le Havre and Cherbourg; in the home airports all the way from Devon to Kent, paratroops, with emergency rations, were already on board the gliders and transport planes which within an hour or two would spill them out all over the Cherbourg Peninsula and the country before Caen. More than a thousand ships of all sizes, from giant liners to dirty tramps and small coastal craft, filled every harbour, packed to their gunwales with machinery and plant for sowing the seeds of freedom on French soil—tanks, guns, ammunition boxes, shells, wagons, medical supplies, food, repair outfits all loaded according to carefully

FIRST STAGE. *Members of the Allied Expeditionary Force wade through the water beside amphibious tanks as they surge ashore to silence enemy positions. Many kinds*

arranged schedules, so that first things might be the first available. Under their hatches nearly a quarter of a million men sprawled and talked and smoked and slept.

Out at sea it was blowing hard, a wind which despite much resistance was to uproot German power and scatter it back across the frontier. For this was the dawn of D-Day, the moment for which countless millions of oppressed people throughout Europe waited and prayed. The Germans, however, knew nothing until the bombs crashed down on their batteries and the parachutists floated to earth. Paratroops seized a couple of bridges near Caen, and held them despite a violent reaction. Some landed in fields, others close to the coast, and collecting themselves, rushed for their immediate objectives. One glider spilled its occupants into the main street of Ste. Mère Eglise, the astonished enemy surrendering without a fight; at other places

fighting was both bitter and bloody.

Meanwhile, before dawn the great armada had got under way, guarded by twin forces of light warships, British under Rear-Admiral Sir Philip Vian on one side, American under Rear-Admiral A. G. Kirk on the other. A special scratch force of small craft acted as a screen against U-boats and E-boats. H.M.SS. *Nelson*, *Warspite* and *Ramillies* lent the weight of their 15 in. and 16 in. guns to the bombardment of almost every place along the Seine Bay, as did three American battleships; and behind this screen landing ships and landing craft passed inshore and discharged tanks and men, often in five feet of water.

The tanks were waterproofed; when they crawled out of the ocean the waterproofing was blown off. General Montgomery, who commanded the operation, had given one comprehensive order, "Don't stop on the beaches, but get inland as far as you can."

of underwater obstacles had to be removed; on the shore concrete forts and barbed wire emplacements formed part of the so-called "Atlantic Wall" built by the Germans.

VICTORIOUS ARMADA. *The extent of the amphibious operations which took the first contingents of Allied troops across the Channel to the beaches of Normandy may be gauged from this photograph, taken shortly before the great fleet of warships, transports, landing craft and supply ships set off on their hazardous mission. The Royal Navy and*

MOPPING UP. *In the country before Cherbourg these American troops are rushing a detachment of Germans who are determined to obey the order, "fight on till death."*

their way in again, and once more had to fall back. Meanwhile the success at Carentan had been pressed home; contact had been established with the British, and the Germans thrust back to their important base at St. Lo.

On June 16, 1944, the 82nd U.S. Airborne Division hurled the enemy from St. Sauveur, on the western road, while the 9th Infantry Brigade passed through the airborne men to fight their way up the west coast at Barneville (June 18). Thus Cherbourg and the country for ten miles inland was isolated.

By-passing Montebourg, the Americans got another pin-point on the coast in the little port of Quineville beyond ; then, after a third bloody struggle in the ruins, regained Monte-

bourg itself. Valogne fell too. The German commander, Lieut.-General von Schlieben, drew in his forces, hoping to hold the fortress.

On June 22, waves of bombers, flying as low as 100 feet, plastered the Germans unmercifully ; next day Tourlaville, a hill only one mile from the harbour, was seized ; but Von Schlieben refused to surrender. His men obeyed fanatically for some days, fighting it out among the ruins in the streets.

The end came on June 27, by which time the Americans had secured more than 20,000 prisoners, though their own losses in killed and wounded were nearly as many. Von Schlieben himself was captured, with Rear-Admiral Hennecke, in a bomb-proof shelter.

PRISON STOCKADE. *Some of the thousands of enemy prisoners who streamed into the emergency prison camps after the fall of Cherbourg are seen in this photograph. They included men from German-occupied countries who had been forced to join the Wehrmacht.*

For these men the war is over, and most of them seem glad to be out of the fighting, in sharp contrast with the sullen visaged Nazis captured earlier in the war. Many more of these camps had to be improvised during the Allied progress towards the Reich.

FIRST REVENGE WEAPON

THE flying bombs were an outstanding instance of the warped Nazi mind. For months a silent war, conducted by the R.A.F., had been waged against German installations near Calais known to be for new robot weapons. The experimental station at Peenemuende had been smashed up, and the commencement of the Nazi revenge attacks constantly postponed. It was London's glory, as well as her misfortune, to be the object of this attack. Citizens of the battered capital met it as stoically as they had endured the earlier blitzing of the city.

Bombing the Sites

The war of the V-bomb—V stood for Vergeltungswaffe, or revenge weapon— began in the autumn of 1943, when the R.A.F. discovered one hundred sites along the French coast with massive concrete structures, the purpose of which could only be guessed. They all pointed towards London.

Thousands of tons of bombs cascaded down on these sites, some of which were destroyed again and again, but the enemy adapted his launching methods sufficiently to send a trial shot on to London on June 13, 1944. Two days later the main V.1 assault began.

The projectile was dubbed "Doodle Bug" by a gun crew, and the name stuck. Its true description, of course, was a pilotless aerial torpedo, jet propelled, with a ton of explosive in its warhead, which rushed through the air at 6½ miles per minute like some evil insect. The noise of the propelling unit ceased, there was an uncomfortable silence of several seconds, then a terrific explosion.

These things were fired at the rate of one hundred a day for seventy-one days on end, and during most nights as well. The record was fifteen warnings within twenty-four hours. General Eisenhower justly called V-bombs damnable things. They were fired at random, sparing neither mansion nor cottage, palace nor prison, big store nor general shop. No military target was ever hit by them, except by one bomb which landed among troops assembled for Divine Service in the beautiful old Guards Chapel. Buckingham Palace, Westminster Hall, the Law Courts, a multiple store, Staple Inn, the Bankruptcy Court, churches, and hospitals, all suffered in some degree.

The wailing of constant alerts proved a severe strain upon the nerves; the sight of maimed people, of bodies on shutters, of scores of little homes smashed to bits, aroused more anger against the Germans than had the earlier attacks on England by the Luftwaffe. Generally speaking, the new weapons accomplished little in the way of interrupting war production.

Defence Measures

At first defence measures proved difficult. The bombs flew so low as to be below the minimum elevation of the guns, and new measures were hastily improvised. From Maidenhead to East Grinstead a huge battery of six hundred A.A. guns was lined up; behind these were 2,000 barrage balloons. On the coast were more gun batteries. The fastest Spitfires, with the new Tempests and Mustangs, flew overhead.

At first one in three got through; by September the ratio was one in eleven and the main danger was over. For a few months the enemy took to launching a few flying bombs by carrier plane over the North Sea.

ALDWYCH DAMAGE. *This photograph shows the destruction caused by a flying bomb which landed at the Aldwych, junction of London's Strand and Fleet Street.*

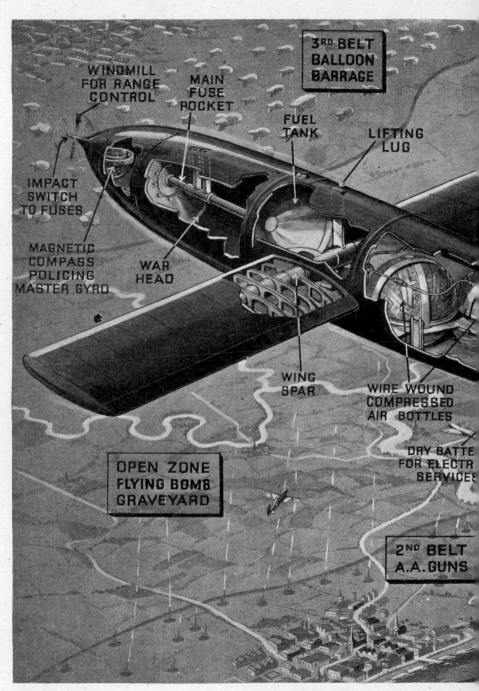

WINDMILL FOR RANGE CONTROL

MAIN FUSE POCKET

3RD BELT BALLOON BARRAGE

FUEL TANK

LIFTING LUG

IMPACT SWITCH TO FUSES

MAGNETIC COMPASS POLICING MASTER GYRO

WAR HEAD

WING SPAR

WIRE WOUND COMPRESSED AIR BOTTLES

DRY BATTE FOR ELECTR SERVICE

OPEN ZONE FLYING BOMB GRAVEYARD

2ND BELT A.A.GUNS

FLYING BOMB DEFENCES. *This impression of a flying bomb and Britain's defences against them shows the great depth of preparations to meet them as they came*

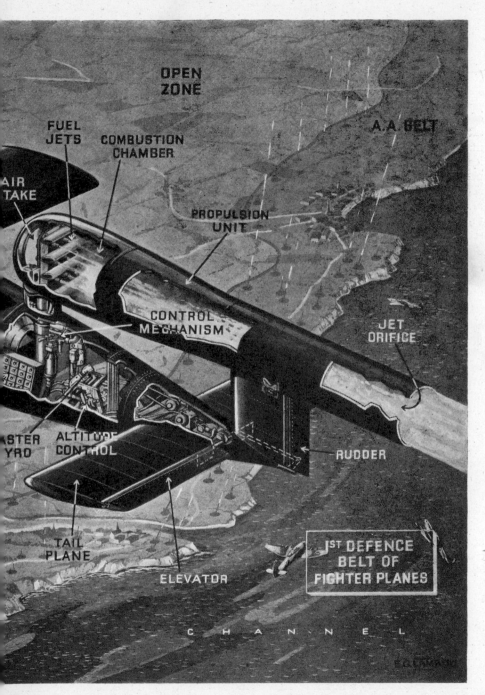

OPEN ZONE

A.A. BELT

FUEL JETS

COMBUSTION CHAMBER

AIR TAKE

PROPULSION UNIT

CONTROL MECHANISM

JET ORIFICE

ASTER YRO

ALTITUDE CONTROL

RUDDER

TAIL PLANE

ELEVATOR

1ST DEFENCE BELT OF FIGHTER PLANES

C H A N N E L

The bombs which escaped being shot down by fighters over the Channel had to run the gauntlet of successive zones of massed barrage balloons and many anti-aircraft guns.

THE CAEN HINGE

THE shattered buildings and debris-littered streets of Caen told more eloquently than words of the value which von Rundstedt attached to this small town in Normandy. The centre of seven trunk roads, it was in fact the enemy's main forward position and the kernel of his resistance. Although only nine miles from the sea, and shelled repeatedly by British naval units, the old town—in ages past the scene of fighting between the French and British—fell only after five weeks of bitter struggle.

When the invasion had sorted itself out, the British occupied Bayeux and part of the road from Bayeux to Caen. On their left, opposite Caen itself, were the Canadians, and on the extreme left the 6th Airborne Division clung tenaciously to the two bridges which kept the enemy from crossing the Orne and Caen canal. Far away on the right the Americans were beginning the operation which cut off the Cherbourg peninsula and liberated the port.

Battleships Bombard the Enemy

The country around and behind Caen is hilly and wooded, much like the county of Devonshire, and admirably suited to defence by pockets of tanks and machine guns. The hills were crowded with Tiger and Panther tanks, 88 mm. guns, booby traps and mines. The British, on the other hand, had tremendously effective flame-throwers, besides the devastating air cover and frequent support from the battleships *Rodney*, *Ramillies* and *Nelson*.

The outstanding feature of the British attack was undoubtedly Field-Marshal Montgomery's famous "right hook," an encircling movement through Tilly and Villers Bocage, in the wooded hills south-west of Caen. Here desperate battles took place over several weeks. The British captured Tilly and Hottot, lost them, captured them again, and again were forced to withdraw temporarily under the enemy pressure.

German Resistance Breaks

A terrific barrage was then systematically built up from guns spaced every five yards, and this finally broke the German resistance, and with it the last enemy hope of beating back the invasion to the sea.

Meanwhile Cherbourg had fallen to the Americans on June 27, and the Allies were assured of a great port through which to pour supplies. The concluding stages of the fight for Caen followed with dramatic suddenness, for the enemy held on until a successful withdrawal became almost a military impossibility. On July 9 the Canadians, pounding their way on through nests of German suicide squads, fought their way into the town, and the grim battle—one of the hardest of the whole war—was ended except for the extermination of fanatical Nazi snipers who still lurked in the ruins of fine old houses and shops.

Bulldozers, the essential followers in the path of modern warfare, came up to clear away the wreckage that littered the streets. The inhabitants of the town came out to welcome their deliverers with a fervour that was undiminished by their personal losses. Throughout the battle they had sheltered in the old Abbey and its cloisters —in touching and justified faith in the amazing accuracy of the Allied bombing and shell-fire. Then began the task of restoring electricity, gas and water to the now liberated countryside.

SOUTH OF CAEN. *Canadians and British fighting on the outskirts of Caen see the explosions from enemy positions as a force of Allied Fortresses are pounding gun sites.*

PRESSURE CONTINUES. *After their brilliant capture of Cherbourg, the Americans began a drive into Brittany which coincided with the British capture of Caen and the drive on to Falaise. By this time the campaign had become one of swift movement and supply, with the fate of the German divisions in France hanging in the balance. As the British and Canadians were trapping thousands of enemy troops in the famous Falaise pocket, the Americans were flooding through to St. Malo and southwards to the Loire.*

Above is shown a small town in north-western France, now consisting of derelict houses clustered round a damaged church. Through the ruins churns the mass of U.S. armour as the broken remnants of the Germans destroy roads and houses left along the path of their retreat. Many towns, broken and battered like this one, were left to mark the last desperate efforts of Hitler's armies to maintain the brutal hold they had kept upon the French countryside since they first marched in during the summer months of 1940.

FALAISE POCKET

THE closure of the Falaise pocket completed the disaster of the German armies in France. "Any enemy unit that managed to get away," wrote General Montgomery to his men, "will not be in a fit condition to fight again for months." The Germans south and south-east of Caen had hung on too long. Rommel was dying, Rundstedt removed, and Kluge, who took over, failed to stem the tide, though at one time his panzers almost cut the Allied armies into two.

At the same time the great southern sweep of the Americans from Avranches to Angers and Nantes, which penned the enemy up in Brest, L'Orient, La Rochelle and St. Malo, was given terrific power by the landing of a new army, the 3rd, under General Patton.

From the west coast of the Cherbourg Peninsula to the Orne the Germans fought back savagely at every hill and cross-road. Nevertheless their front crumbled and finally dissolved. American spearheads swept down to the Loire, General Patton turned east and north, through Le Mans and Alençon, to Argentan, a few miles from the Canadians at Falaise. The French patriots, armed with Sten guns dropped by parachute, helped materially by disorganizing the enemy's communications.

Kluge decided to pull out, but it was too late. His columns, crowding every road to the east, were battered to destruction by Typhoons, bombers and artillery. On August 16, 1944, the Falaise pocket was only six miles wide; two days later it had narrowed to two miles ; on the 19th it was closed.

FALL OF CAEN. *These British soldiers survey the ruins of Caen after the enemy has been finally driven out of this town.*

FREE AGAIN. *As the Anglo-American forces bit more deeply into German occupied territory, thousands of Frenchmen now found themselves liberated from the German yoke.*

This happy group shows typical French working folk greeting their liberators. The little girl had never known freedom before Allied armour chased the enemy from her home.

ACTION IN THE SOUTH

WHILE von Kluge's armies, with ten of their generals dead, were still reeling back towards the Seine in a vain attempt to get out of the Falaise pocket, the Allies struck yet another blow, seven hundred miles away, but sufficiently near to prove, once and for all, how hollow a sham was Hitler's "Fortress of Europe."

At dawn on August 15 an armada of ships landed American, French and British troops at Fréjus and other small Mediterranean ports between Cannes and Toulon. The invasion, which was prefaced by several days of aerial battering, took place under the smoke of a sharp warship bombardment. It was preceded by clouds of U.S. and British paratroops dropping from the skies.

The Germans had their forces hopelessly scattered, and in any case their numbers were inadequate to hold the mountainous and wholly hostile district of Provence. Within ten days the American 7th Army, under Lieut.-General Patch, was in Grenoble. In those same ten days Paris was liberated by the French Forces of the Interior, General Patton was threatening Verdun, General Hodges was on the Meuse, and General Montgomery had brought his forces to the Somme.

In the south, General Patch's forces, to which the French had added an army under General Delattre de Tassigny, rolled forward irresistibly, preceded by the inevitable air cover. Only at Toulon, Marseilles, Hyères, and on some islands near Cannes was opposition serious. In the hilly country towards the French Alps the invaders had but to march to conquer, for here the French Maquis had maintained a flame of revolt (especially in Savoy) which even German cruelties had never quite extinguished during the occupation.

PATH OF GERMAN RETREAT. *Floods and bomb craters disfigure the Rhône valley.*

Preceded by strong forces of Allied bombers the armies which had landed in the south chased confused masses of enemy troops more than 600 miles towards the Reich frontier.

TIDE OF FREEDOM

As the French patriots rose against the oppressors, German prisoners surrendered in the south by tens of thousands. In the first ten days after August 15, 19,000 Germans had been taken; the French had smashed two divisions holding Toulon and Marseilles, and Col.-General Blaskowitz, the enemy commander, was trying desperately to get his troops up the Rhône Valley towards Lyons.

At Toulon port, the devastation wrought by the enemy was terrible, with the harbour full of sunken ships. Marseilles escaped more lightly. But no measures of this sort could stop the U.S. 3rd, 26th and 45th Infantry Divisions as they rattled and bumped northwards along the bad roads. They streamed through Avignon, through Montélimar, through Valence. By the end of the month, prisoners reached 50,000. The ancient town of Vienne, twenty miles from Lyons, was liberated on September 2, 1944, and Lyons itself the following day. Wrecking the bridges over the Rhône, von Blaskowitz urged his tired and demoralized men northwards, but the pursuers stuck to them grimly. By September 7, when the Germans, on nearing the Belfort Gap into Alsace, turned and struck back fiercely, the 3rd Army had covered 700 miles from their landing places on the Mediterranean, a record even for mechanized warfare.

Vichy, and all that the Vichy regime of Marshal Pétain stood for, had fallen. Pétain, Laval, and lesser men had wisely fled with the enemy. The tide of freedom was to pursue them into the Greater Reich itself and bring them back to face their countrymen.

THE VANQUISHED. *Still arrogant, but now quite harmless, 20,000 prisoners start to stream along the lanes of southern France.*

PARIS REJOICES. *The great crowds which throng the Paris boulevards give the American forces and the French army under General Leclerc a tumultuous welcome as they march through the streets of France's recently freed capital. The German garrison have hurriedly capitulated and the main enemy forces are streaming back across the Seine.*

The sound of rifle shots was still occasionally heard above the cheering as a few German Nazis and French fascists continued to snipe at the crowds from the windows of buildings. This continued for a week until the French authorities, aided by the men of the F.F.I., steadily "winkled them out." French collaborators were seized and held for trial.

DRIVE INTO BELGIUM

O<small>N</small> August 20, 1944, but a single day after the Falaise gap had been closed, General Patton's troops were within 21 miles of Paris, which they threatened from Versailles in the west and Fontainebleau in the south. Within the capital itself a revolt had already broken out. The F.F.I., fifty thousand strong, were aided by the police who were on strike. The Ile de la Cité was seized and Nôtre Dame surrounded.

Enemy tanks were fired or bombed, machine guns captured, and in a series of street fights the Germans were hurled out of most public buildings, including the Hôtel de Ville. After several days of this, on August 24, the French 2nd Armoured Division, under General Leclerc, entered the city at 8 a.m. Paris was French again.

A few hours afterwards part of the U.S. Tank Division followed. There ensued a fierce man-hunt, German snipers and a few French fascists defending isolated buildings to the last. When General de Gaulle, who was in France, entered Paris, he was greeted by bullets as well as the cheering of his compatriots. The German Commander, Scholtitz, agreed to surrender.

By August 27, American and Canadian troops had crossed the Seine in great force, and the British, from their bridgehead at Vernon, on the Seine, covered the 206 miles to Brussels, capital of Belgium, in six days, against steady opposition. As Montgomery's men entered the city, flags draped the buildings, and thousands of voices sang " Tipperary " and other songs, remembered from the days of 1914-18.

BRUSSELS GOES WILD. *Songs of 1914-18 greeted the British troops as they proudly marched through the capital.*

HEROISM AT ARNHEM

THE stand of the British 1st Paratroop Division at Arnhem ranks among the greatest achievements of the British Army. The attack itself was a risk taken in the knowledge that its success would shorten the war by many vital months, with a consequent saving of thousands of valuable lives.

The British were advancing into Holland from the south, entering a country bad in autumn for tank warfare, with sticky mud, numerous floods (these heightened by the German policy of flooding the countryside), and large, deep streams that ran across the route. A crossing of the River Maas had been forced, but beyond the river the enemy held the town of Eindhoven in the open plain; beyond Eindhoven were the two main branches of the Rhine, the Waal and the Lek, both great rivers spanned by steel bridges.

What Was Planned

On the near side of the Waal lay Nijmegen ; five miles to the north was the little town of Elst ; five miles beyond that flows the Lek, on the farther bank of which stood Arnhem. It was decided to drop many thousands of paratroops to seize Nijmegen, Eindhoven and Arnhem. With these crossings gained, British armour would then rush across the bridges, fan out into Westphalia, and thus with one stroke turn the defence system that protected western Germany. On September 17, 1944, this plan was attempted.

The great aerial armada that streamed out from airfields in Britain on that brilliant September day carried more paratroops than had ever been seen before in one air-borne operation. Eindhoven fell fairly easily, but Nijmegen yielded only after a sharp struggle. The operation was carried out like clockwork. The aircraft and gliders landed with their loads or dropped their paratroops dead to schedule. Some of the gliders carried light guns, jeeps, and small tanks. Their arrival was witnessed by Dutch civilians, many of whom were returning from church.

Simultaneously spearheads of the British army moved forward across the Dutch frontier; the whole point of the scheme was that the link-up between the main army and the air-borne men should be effected without delay. By 10 a.m. on September 18, troops of the British Second Army had made contact with the air-borne troops at Eindhoven, and on the 20th they were smashing through to the River Waal, north-east of Nijmegen, as the city itself was the scene of a furious battle. Huge glider trains, filling the sky for 285 miles, swept out of Britain with reinforcements, with the great Halifaxes and Stirlings acting as tow-planes.

Heavy and Hopeless Fighting

Meanwhile the Germans were reacting with furious determination. At Arnhem, about 6,500 men had floated down by parachute and succeeded in gaining control of the bridge, together with an area about two miles square. By day and night they experienced frantic enemy counter attacks. The time factor began to turn against them, for the main British forces, advancing from Nijmegen, encountered impenetrable enemy resistance at Elst. On September 23, thousands of British and American glider-borne troops were dropped in support of the British Second Army's efforts to relieve the

TENSE MOMENT AT ARNHEM. *Outwardly peaceful, the quiet Dutch countryside is the scene of heated battle. Paratroops equipped with light jeeps make haste to secure ammunition dropped by parachute before the Germans can organize a counter attack.*

Arnhem men. At the same time the Germans made repeated efforts to cut the Allied corridor to Nijmegen.

Apart from some of the Dorsets and a few Poles, no reinforcements reached the paratroops; the R.A.F., in bad weather, continued to take frightful risks to drop supplies but steadily the tiny garrison were being decimated as the Germans, recovered from their first shock, rushed up tanks, mortars, and self-propelled guns. Eventually the airborne men were split up into small bodies, still fighting, but with the enemy ring round them slowly contracting. By September 25 it was apparent that the bid had failed, and that there could be no link-up between the main army and the vanguard at Arnhem. During the nights of the 25th and 26th, the survivors slipped through the enemy lines and were taken back in boats. Two thousand eight hundred were evacuated, and 1,200 wounded had to be left behind. Such was the epic and glory of the Arnhem bridgehead, and though the battles which were fought around the small Dutch town were fought in vain, they added an immortal page to the history of British arms and the indomitable men who bore them.

UNDER FIRE. *This photograph was taken during the fourth day of bitter fighting at Arnhem. Tired, grimy paratroopers unpack supplies dropped by the R.A.F. as the counter attack against them grows steadily sharper and relief is still far away.*

As the action continued and the British were still isolated, the Allied air forces took desperate risks in visibility which made flying hazardous to drop fresh supplies of much-needed food, medical supplies and ammunition to men fighting on the ground.

JUNKERS TURN ON HITLER

ON July 20, 1944, the Junker leaders of the German Army made an attempt to rid themselves of the domination of the Nazi Party. This attempt was not caused by any belated fondness for democratic institutions, but as an attempt at self-preservation in the disasters the professional soldiers saw clearly were ahead.

For months the German generals captured by the Russians had issued appeals over the radio to the Wehrmacht to abandon Hitler. At the beginning of 1944, Major-Gen. von Treskow had suggested to a colleague, Major-Gen. Stieff, that the Fuehrer should be assassinated by explosives at a military conference. This idea was worked into a plot by General Olbricht, an ambitious Junker who was second in command of the Home Army, and was stationed in Berlin. Other leaders in the affair were Colonel-General Beck, formerly Chief-of-Staff before his dismissal by Hitler, Colonel-General Hoeppner, and Field-Marshal Witzleben. These three men had nothing further to gain by supporting the Nazis in prolonging the war.

Bomb in Dispatch Case

The assassin was Colonel Count Stauffenberg, who managed to obtain entry to Hitler's headquarters on July 20, shortly before noon. Present in the room, besides Hitler himself, were several highly-placed staff officers. Stauffenberg had concealed the bomb in a dispatch case, which he placed casually on the floor near Hitler's feet before making an excuse to leave. After a moment or two the bomb exploded, hurling some of the occupants of the room out of the window. In the belief that his mission had been successful, Stauffenberg rushed to Berlin in a waiting courier aircraft, and reported to Hoeppner that Hitler was dead.

Hoeppner, using orders which Witzleben had prepared, commanded the Berlin Guards to occupy all Government buildings, but the commander, Major Remer, cautiously rang up Goebbels to verify his orders. Goebbels immediately placed him in telephone contact with Hitler, and the plot was still-born.

Hitler had a miraculous escape. His stenographer was killed, and the officers round him severely injured, but in a few hours the familiar voice of the Fuehrer was heard denouncing the plotters over the radio.

Field-Marshal Witzleben and Colonel-General Beck, knowing all was lost, attempted to seize the Berlin Broadcasting Station, but were beaten back by the Guards. Beck shot himself, Witzleben was arrested, and the miserable Stauffenberg was seized, tried, and shot within an hour. Dr. Goerdeler, Chief Burgomaster of Leipzig, who was to have been the new Reichs-Chancellor (with Beck as Commander-in-Chief and Witzleben as Chief-of-Staff) disappeared from his home.

Himmler and his S.S. made a rapid round-up of all Army elements suspected of being in the plot. A People's Court was set up, with several members of the Wehrmacht as judges of their fellow officers. Most of the conspirators were rounded up, sentenced, and executed with great cruelty a few hours afterwards. So ended the last attempt by the German aristocracy to unseat the Nazi Party. Hitler remained as the German Leader, with the sinister figure of Himmler as chief executive.

GESTAPO TAKES OVER. *Heinrich Himmler, head of the Gestapo, took over German armed forces after the failure of the Hitler assassination attempt. (Above), he reviews S.S. men fighting in the west. (Below), wearing soft hats and "civvies" members of the Volkssturm—German equivalent of the Home Guard—march past a saluting base in Berlin.*

HITLER'S ROCKET OFFENSIVE

DURING the October and November of 1944, the Nazis put into effect their second secret weapon—the device known as the rocket bomb or V.2. For many weeks no official mention was made of the new attack, and this calculated secrecy effectively prevented the enemy from gaining precise information of the effect of the new weapon, which penetrated deeper and had a greater local effect than the flying bomb, which now made its appearance over London very seldom.

The missile was a more ingenious and deadly thing than the flying bomb. Its flight could not be intercepted, it made a hole 30 ft. deep, and usually shattered everything where it fell. On the other hand, it was far less accurate than the V.1, and fell anywhere between Southend and Reading. The fact, too, that it burst without warning detracted from its "terror" effect.

How They Worked

Rocket bombs were altogether larger than the V.1. The shape resembled a giant torpedo, 46 ft. long and 5 ft. in diameter, with no outside parts except four fins in the tail. The rocket's long, pointed nose contained 2,000 lb. of explosive, behind which was a small compartment containing control gear and a radio device. Next came a large aluminium tank, holding about 7,500 gallons of alcohol; and behind that a second tank with 11,000 lb. of liquid oxygen. These tanks made up most of the body; behind them was a turbine, driven by a gas generator, and in the stern a stoutly constructed combustion chamber and two sets of control vanes.

Rockets needed only a small platform for launching, a feature which made the launching sites difficult to destroy. Before firing the rocket stood vertically. The turbine drove a pump, forcing liquid oxygen and alcohol through jets into the combustion chamber. The mixture, electrically ignited, forced out hot, rapidly expanding gases so fiercely as to give an upward thrust of about 26 tons, sufficient to push the rocket forward at a tremendous rate, nearly twice as fast as that of a shell from a gun.

Hurtling Through Space

A gyroscope brought the control vanes into play, and the missile curved towards its target, the fuel supply being cut off one minute after launching. As the rocket fell, friction made its outer covering red-hot, and many exploded harmlessly in mid-air, possibly from this cause.

On impact, a double explosion occurred, the second noise being that of the rush of displaced air during the descent of the missile, the sound of which reached those on the ground after that of the explosion. Most of them were fired from Holland, with a range of about 200 miles, though some came from Westphalia. The distance was covered in roughly five minutes, the rocket ascending to heights of 60 to 70 miles.

People in England had no sooner congratulated themselves on being rid of the flying bomb menace, when this new terror confronted them. Little could be done by the Allied Air Forces, particularly as the Germans launched them from closely populated parts of Holland. Rockets had to be endured until the thrusting Allied Armies hurled the Germans back over the Rhine and out of occupied Holland.

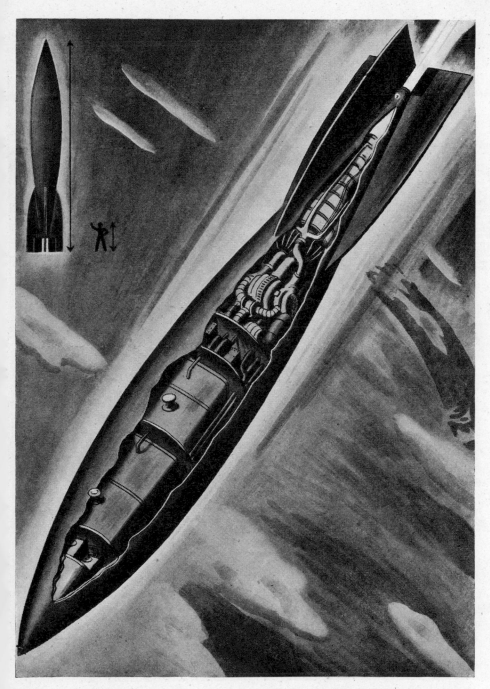

ROCKET IN FLIGHT. *Specially commissioned for this book, the above is an impression of the rocket bomb in flight. Top left is shown the rocket in relation to a man's height.*

IN THE STREETS OF BREST. *Fumes and smoke from explosives fill the narrow streets of Brest, where 12,000 members of the German garrison gave in on September 19, 1944.*

PURSUIT FROM THE AIR. *These B-17 Flying Fortresses of the U.S. Eighth Air Force release their bombs in a cascade during relentless precision bombing of the fleeing enemy.*

BRITISH MOVE UP. *Through the snow which has fallen on the western front, British infantry move into the great Ardennes salient caused by Rundstedt's offensive.*

WEHRMACHT'S LAST THROW

By mid-December, 1944, the Rhine and Cologne were directly threatened by the U.S. Ninth Army, under General Simpson, and the First Army, under General Hodges. North of Simpson the British and Canadians were waterlogged on the Maas; south of Hodges the Third Army, under General Patton, were fighting a life-or-death struggle in Dillingen, Saarlautern and Sarreguemines. South of Patton the U.S. Seventh Army and the French were almost across Alsace. To stop this flood the German Commander, Rundstedt, decided to risk everything in a furious counter offensive.

Hidden by winter mists and rains two Panzer armies and a Grenadier army were assembled, equipped with first-class weapons, including high velocity 88mm. guns, Royal Tiger tanks, and flame throwers. At dawn on December 16, 1944, German armour burst on the weakest part of Hodges' First Army, between Trèves and Dueren. Four great columns struck a gap in the American lines, sixty miles wide. In the north the enemy streamed through at Monschau, in the centre they approached Bastogne, and in the south they swept across northern Luxembourg. They were only kept out of Luxembourg city by a scratch force of Americans.

By Christmas Day the Germans were within four miles of the Meuse and more than fifty into Belgium. General Eisenhower placed his armies which lay north of the break-through under Field-Marshal Montgomery, who had already moved his troops up to meet the attack. At Celles and Ciney, British and Americans, fighting as one team, halted the foe; by December 27 the worst was over. Mid-January saw fierce strokes by the British in the north and by Patton's Third Army in the south hurl the Germans back to their original positions. Up to January 17, 1945, the Americans had lost 40,000 men, and the enemy 90,000.

TIGHT CORNER. *These Americans are seen engaged in a bitter struggle against advancing enemy infantry during the last great German offensive of the war.*

THEIR OWN MEDICINE. *After ten days of fighting, Aachen fell on October 20, 1944, the town itself being transformed into a heap of rubble and smashed buildings.*

eeping from cellars where they had huddled, German civilians clambered over the eckage of their homes, all of them loud in complaints against Hitler and the Nazis.

ALLIES SMASH THROUGH

O N February 23, 1945, the Canadian First Army, British Second Army and American First and Ninth Armies, preceded by all the typical Montgomery technique—thorough preparation, smokescreens, a devastating artillery barrage, and a heavy air umbrella—opened a general attack from Nijmegen to Venlo. "We are going," said General Eisenhower, "to destroy every German west of the Rhine." This was no mere threat. The Americans, swarming across the Ruhr, captured Julich and Dueren, and by the 28th had taken Munchen-Gladbach and were shelling Cologne. The Canadians, despite intense opposition, struck north from the Maas through Calcar and Udem; while the British aimed at the Wesel crossing.

In the south General Patton's Third Army systematically hacked their way through the maze of Siegfried Line fortifications around Trèves. Everywhere battle was joined, a battle that raged until the Germans were forced back to the Rhine, broken and bewildered. Many of the enemy got across, many were drowned, others tamely gave in.

Cologne Falls

At Xanten, near the Wesel crossing, there was a desperate struggle against German paratroops; but the First Somerset Light Infantry brilliantly captured this important point. Krefeld, Neuss, Cologne, Bonn, all were taken, and by March 10, 1945, the Allies held a continuous stretch of the Rhine from Nijmegen for almost 150 miles, or nearly to Coblenz. At this point twenty-four German divisions had been destroyed or hopelessly battered.

The Germans had always regarded the Rhine as their safest frontier, and its swift-flowing waters are a formidable barrier. But Remagen Bridge, between Bonn and Coblenz, fell into American hands. At 3.50 p.m. on March 8 an advanced patrol of the American Ninth Army reached the bridge, disconnected the fuses attached to the mines, and crossed to the further bank. Soon tanks and infantry were roaring over, and by March 11 this vital bridgehead was ten miles wide and five miles deep. The enemy succeeded in hitting the bridge from the air, but by that time the Americans had built a strong pontoon bridge, over which men and transport passed unhindered.

Montgomery Crosses the Rhine

No other Rhine crossing was attempted until the night of March 22, when General Patton's men made a spectacular crossing at Oppenheim, near Mainz. Next day, under cover of a billowing smoke screen, Field-Marshal Montgomery's men passed over at Wesel. These three crossings, aided by Allied paratroops, were followed by the building of many pontoon bridges. For a few days the hard crust of German resistance remained, then the German armies commenced to disintegrate before the immense pressure of men and arms against them.

Meanwhile day after day, in brilliant April sunshine, the Allied bombers pounded away at the head of the advance columns. The Luftwaffe, grounded for want of petrol, lost 1,738 planes in a fortnight. In the air as well as on the ground, the game was up for Germany, and the end of the war in the west was within sight, for the Allied armies now had no great natural obstacles in their path, and the German armies could not stand up to them.

BATTLEFIELD. (*Top*) *A dead German sprawls in the mire near a wrecked field kitchen.* (*Bottom*) *An American has shot first in an encounter with a German sniper.*

SHRIVELLING FLAME. *A British Churchill tank, equipped for flame-throwing, lumbers up to enemy positions. Great tongues of scorching fire sear the earth in its path.*

Weapons such as these, better than any the Germans could oppose, hurled the enemy back to their last bastion, the Rhine. Even here they could not halt the Allied advance.

THIS WAS COLOGNE. *Only the great Gothic cathedral stands undestroyed amid the devastation and carnage that was once a great German city. It fell on March 6, 1945.*

The capture of Cologne symbolized the impotence of the German High Command to pre-
vent the Allies from pressing on across the Rhine into the heart of Hitler's Reich itself.

JUMPING THE RHINE. *Above is shown part of a regiment of the 17th U.S. Airborne Division jumping on to the further bank of the Rhine from their huge transport planes.*

THEY ARRIVE. *One of the paratroopers crouches down as he helps a wounded comrade. Hundreds have landed in this vast air operation far into enemy-held territory.*

BRITISH FREE BURMA

ON March 7, 1945, Major-General Rees's 19th Indian Division, after advancing eighteen miles in twenty-four hours, stormed into Mandalay City. On April 10 Rangoon was captured, and the Japanese stranglehold upon Burma had been broken.

The earlier deeds of the heroic forces in Burma had been somewhat overshadowed by events in Europe and the Middle East, but quietly and competently an immensely difficult and long campaign had been planned and executed successfully in forest and mountain country that was the worst possible for white troops to operate in.

India Threat Smashed

When Admiral Lord Louis Mountbatten was appointed C.-in-C. of S.E. Asia Command it was expected that amphibious operations at Akyab and other ports would be used to break the Japanese in Burma. Two events upset this plan—although Arakan was successfully invaded. These were : the fact that Europe had priority for landing craft, and the bold Japanese bid to drive on to India. Three strong enemy columns advanced by jungle roads into Manipur and north-east Assam, country where civilization was scarce. Considerable British forces were surrounded at Imphal and Kohima, but they were supplied from the air and held their own in jungle-fighting.

Relieving forces, assisted by guerilla activity behind the Japanese lines, forced the enemy to withdraw. All this occurred during the height of the monsoon, when Assam is one of the wettest countries in the world.

The British then developed a great air transport service. Weapons, ammunition, light armour, and reinforcements, totalling 70,000 tons of supplies and 93,000 men, were flown from India; 25,000 wounded and sick were flown back. Casualties were not heavy, but nearly a quarter of a million malaria cases were evacuated. The ground supply line was almost inconceivable—up one mountain and down another—and but for the bulldozers would have been impossible to negotiate at all.

Japanese Fall Back

Meanwhile other troops were fighting on the upper Chindwin and (with Chinese aid) near the Burma Road. By the end of the monsoon (mid-October, 1944) the British were pushing the Japanese along several parallel lines, the Chindwin in the west, the main Irrawaddy from Katha to Mandalay, and the upper Irrawaddy. British county regiments and the cream of the Indian army were engaged in this task.

On January 7, 1945, one column broke into Sheebo, fifty miles north of Mandalay; on January 17 the river was crossed only thirty miles from the city. On February 14 and 24 two other columns, who had marched south through dense jungle, seized the town of Meiktila, far below Mandalay. Their line of retreat now threatened, the Japanese gave the order for a general retreat. The hold that they had established in 1942 had been smashed.

On May 5, 1945, Lord Louis Mountbatten announced that, with the capture of Rangoon by the 14th Army, the Burma campaign was concluded. He added, " The liberation of Burma, in which we have had the active assistance of the Burmese, marks not only the successful accomplishment of the first stage . . . It will also be your springboard for further and greater victories."

ACTION IN BURMA. *Sherman and Lee tanks rumble along a dried river bed in central Burma towards a reported enemy outpost during the drive to Mandalay in 1945.*

RUSSIANS PRESS ON

FROM August, 1944, when the Germans had been driven from most Soviet territory, until the end of the European war in May, 1945, great blows were dealt by the Red Army against the Wehrmacht. Most of the Soviet generals in the field were young men, but their armies were welded into one strategic whole by the genius of Marshal Stalin and his general staff. By the Russian plan Germany itself was assailed through Poland into Prussia, and through Roumania (which capitulated to Russia in August, 1944) and Hungary into Austria and Czecho-Slovakia.

Marshal Tolbukhin's men occupied the whole north bank of the Danube up to the Iron Gates. The Germans were ejected from Yugoslavia. By October the Russians were pouring across the Hungarian plain towards Budapest, while another army were fighting their way down the Carpathian passes from the north. At the same time Tolbhukin,

coming up on the other bank of the Danube, completed the surrounding of the Hungarian capital. Realizing that if Budapest fell, then Vienna would soon be invested, the Germans made stupendous efforts to break the Russian ring round the city. Several times they tried, and at least once got within sight of the city, but always they failed to link up with the trapped German forces.

Within Budapest a fight nearly as grim as Stalingrad ensued, ending with the annihilation of the German garrison by February 13, 1945.

Elsewhere Stalin maintained constant pressure. By mid-October, 1944, Chernyakhovsky made a fierce onslaught on East Prussia via Gumbinnen. He was halted for a time by a fortified zone. Then on January 12, 1945, two more Russian armies, commanded by Koniev and Zhukov, were unleashed simultaneously. They tore the defence to ribbons and in eleven days had fought their way through to the River

VIENNA. *Surrounded by the Russian armies the Nazi garrison in the Austrian capital were speedily mopped up. Austrian anti-fascists helped the Red Army in their operations.*

BUDAPEST. *In the heart of the Hungarian capital Russian tanks and infantry blast houses still held by the Germans after the relief attempts have been finally beaten off.*

Oder. Warsaw, which the Russians had just failed to reach the previous summer when the Polish patriots had risen under General Bor, fell on January 17. By the 21st Cracow and Tilsit saw Russian tanks and self-propelled guns rolling through the streets. Two German strongpoints in Poznan and Breslau were bypassed, and the defenders of East Prussia were pressed back against the Baltic coast, separate groups holding out for a time at Elbing, Koenigsberg and Danzig.

On February 11, 1945, a crossing of the Oder was forced, and with this went the last German hope of holding the Red Army to a stalemate. Koniev had pressed far in German Silesia, and Frankfort and Cuestrin were systematically enveloped. In these vital days the German position was everywhere deteriorating. In Austria Marshal Tolbhukin and Marshal Malinovsky were converging upon Vienna. In the west the

Germans were retreating in a confused mass over the Rhine. It was now that the American, British, and Russian armies commenced to deliver knock-out blows from all directions upon the territory still under German control.

The road to Berlin was covered by Zhuhov's men, while Vienna was suffering the same fate as Budapest. The Austrian capital was invested first when Malinovsky closed the last escape route on April 11. Inside nine days the city had fallen, Austrian anti-fascists aiding the Red Army in their task. In Czecho-Slovakia a Russian army was approaching the capital of Prague, where the patriots were preparing to have their reckoning with the garrison.

On April 26, 1945, the historic meeting took place at Torgau, in the heart of Germany between advanced American and Russian patrols. It had been a long, hard road, but the Russians had now reached the end of it.

THE REICH DISINTEGRATES

APRIL 2, 1945, found General Dempsey's men racing away one hundred miles from the Rhine, heading across north-west Germany. At the same time Generals Simpson and Hodges succeeded in capturing Paderborn, behind the Ruhr, thus cutting off an immense industrial area with nearly 100,000 enemy troops inside the net.

To the south, General Patton's tough veterans poured towards Cassel from captured Frankfort. South of these, General Patch's Seventh Army was at Wurtzburg after severe fighting. This army, which had entered France through the Rhône Valley, and had passed across Alsace, was destined within the month to sweep through Nuremberg, Salzburg, the Tyrol, and to join up with Field-Marshal Alexander's armies in Italy. On April 5, the French, in at the kill, crossed the Rhine below Basle and thereby pinned down many fleeing Germans against the Swiss frontier.

Key Points Fall

It was an avalanche that no army in the world could have stopped, let alone the Germans, already fearful of defeat. The enemy were utterly bewildered as the Allied armies advanced under cover of a news " blackout." They fought fiercely enough for key points like Bremen, Wurtzburg, Nuremberg and Leipzig, but there was no co-ordination in their direction. Thousands of them wandered across country, seeking any Allied soldier who would accept their surrender.

By April 10, the British, headed by the famous "Desert Rats", had taken Minden and were heading for Hamburg and Bremen; at Bremen the Germans resisted like trapped animals, but Hamburg fell with scarcely a struggle.

On the British left, the Canadians, striking northward towards the Zuyder Zee, reached Groningen on the North Sea by April 16 and thus cut off Holland. On this day General Patton had reached Chemnitz, in the heart of Saxony; while Koniev chose the same moment to throw the Russian armies across the Oder towards the suburbs of Berlin.

As General Patch reached Nuremberg on April 19, the First Army battled into Leipzig, where prominent Nazis committed suicide with their families. Simultaneously the Ninth Army, which for a week had been on the Elbe, swooped down on Magdeburg, and then waited until the Russians arrived for the historic meeting of the Allies on April 26.

Wholesale Surrender

Far away to the north the British, finally smothering Bremen, and taking Hamburg in their stride, streamed north to the Baltic coast. Then, on May 3, 1945, nearly a million Germans, the whole force occupying Germany, Holland and Denmark, surrendered to Field-Marshal Montgomery unconditionally at Luneburg. Similar disaster had overtaken the enemy's Italian armies after the British offensive across the Senio had smashed them at Bologna. On April 29 another million had surrendered to Field-Marshal Alexander, including those in the Tyrol, almost to the front door of Berchtesgaden. On May 6, 250,000 more surrendered to the Americans. Nothing remained of the Third Reich but a few fighting fragments, the ruins of their towns, the bodies of their dead, and the lasting shame of their evil deeds.

LAST JOURNEY. *Citizens of Washington see the funeral cortege of their great President passing through the streets of the capital, escorted by members of the services.*

part in the resistance to the march of the Axis powers.

When Britain and France went to the aid of Poland, President Roosevelt voiced the opinions of the vast majority of his countrymen when he denounced the aggression of Hitler that had caused the war. At the same time America, in pursuance of its Constitution, enforced a rigorous neutrality. This was relaxed in the autumn of that year, as a result of the President's inspired advocacy, to permit "cash and carry" purchases by the Allies. Later, when Allied credits and ships grew short, this principle was extended into "Lease Lend."

In December, 1941, .the Japanese hurled themselves on America's Pacific possessions, and America joined the Allies. Then the President became a tower of strength indeed. His meetings with Churchill and Stalin forged plans that led to the landings in Africa, Italy and France. Millions of American men came to Europe to fight: in the Far East British and American resources were used against the Japanese as one.

During most of his career President Roosevelt was crippled from the waist down. No consideration of personal comfort prevented him from travelling thousands of miles to plan, negotiate, and inspect in the Allied cause. So continued his career of public duty until he died—a few days before the collapse of Hitler's Germany.

In his own country he was called the greatest President since Abraham Lincoln. From all parts of the world poured tributes. From Winston Churchill came Britain's own tribute in the words: ". . . . in Franklin Roosevelt died the greatest American friend we have ever known."

305

THIS WAS THE WEHRMACHT. *German prisoners filled vast enclosures as more and still more men in uniform, from generals to privates, came to surrender.*

From a trickle of a few hundred, prisoners grew into thousands and then tens of thousands each day. Each new influx placed increasing strain on Allied administration.

VICTIMS OF THE NAZIS

As the curtain of German occupation was pushed back by the Allied armies clear evidence of sub-human cruelty upon an enormous scale was revealed. A large number of cases and incidents were fully documented by Allied commissions with sworn statements by witnesses and photographs, forming a permanent record that could never be dismissed by German apologists as being faked " war propaganda."

Apart from the execution and confinement of democrats, communists and " intellectuals " from their own and occupied countries, the Germans attempted the systematic extermina-tion of the European Jews. For this purpose Poland was used as an execution centre, to which Jews of many nationalities were brought. In 1942 Himmler, after a stay in Warsaw, ordered that one-half the Polish Jews were to be killed in the course of one year. Six to seven thousand people were removed daily by a Vernichtungs-kommando (Extermination Squad) of picked thugs.

In Yugoslavia 85,000 Jews were killed by various methods ; 20,000 Jews were executed in one day in the Russian town of Lutsk ; 75,000 Jews were deported from Slovakia to the Polish ghettoes up to the end of 1942.

A FEW OF THE VICTIMS. *Shown below is one of the rough communal graves of Belsen concentration camp into which the dead and nearly dead were thrown by the Nazis.*

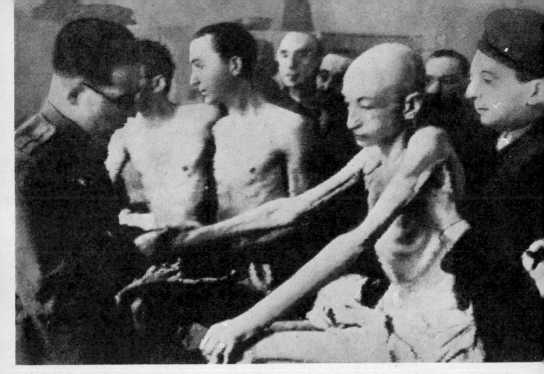

LIVING SKELETON. *A Russian medical officer is seen examining a young Viennese, one of many similar cases discovered by the Red Army in a Silesian death camp.*

These few statistics give an idea of the completeness of the Nazi campaign.

It was, however, within the frontiers of Germany itself that the most horrible sights were discovered. The great Nazi concentration camps of Buchenwald, Dachau, Belsen and the like were overrun by the Allies and discovered to be crammed with thousands of half-starved, disease-ridden wrecks of men progressed beyond human aid.

A delegation from the British Parliament were rushed to Buchenwald to prepare a report. Speed was necessary because of the mass of swiftly decomposing bodies that piled up every day.

The delegation reported that inmates calculated the total number of deaths in the camp since January, 1945, as 51,572. "The mortuary block," states the official White Paper of the visit, "consisted of two floors, ground floor and basement. Access to the basement was by a steep stone staircase or by a vertical chute below a trap door, down either of which, we were told, refractory or useless prisoners would be precipitated for execution. Hanging appears to have been the regular method of killing. In the yard, near a pile of white ashes, there was a gibbet; in the basement we saw strong hooks, at a height of about 8 ft. from the floor, and another gibbet . . . We were shown a heavy wooden club, about 2 ft. long, which was said to have been used for knocking out any who died slowly; it was stained with blood."

In the camp itself the huts consisted of small cubicles, 6 ft. in depth, in which five to six men had to sleep—Buchenwald was in the main for men and boys. For bedclothes they had such rags as they could collect. They were, inevitably, verminous; what was worse, dysentery and typhoid were rife . . . The dead were pushed out into the gangways by the living . . . "

DEAD AND DISHONOURED. *The bodies of Benito Mussolini and his mistress hang upside down in Milan after their execution by Italian partisans on April 28, 1945.*

IN THE DUST. *A framed photograph of the Fuehrer lies in the rubble ; with the advance of the Allies Hitler vanished from the scene and was announced as dead.*

THE END IN THE WEST

SWIFT and dramatic was the collapse of Germany in the April and early May of 1945. Assailed from all sides, what remained of German strategy was to stem the Russian advance at all costs ; while individual commanders of the isolated armies in the west were instructed to fight on to the last against the British and Americans to gain time.

Berlin was, in Stalin's phrase, " the heart of German aggression," and it was in the capital, once the home of four million people, that crack enemy troops, mostly fanatical Nazis, were assembled, backed by the Volkssturm and heartened by daily appeals from Hitler and Goebbels, who had made the city their headquarters. The many cellars and air-raid shelters were turned into strongpoints, sewers and the underground railway became links between the various improvised fortresses and dumps.

Nevertheless, when Marshals Zhukov and Koniev made their all-out attack, Berlin lasted three weeks before street fighting finished on May 2. The city was pounded into a ghastly welter of destruction as Russian tanks and dive-bombers ploughed a course through the suburbs to the centre. The enemy fought resolutely, but nothing could stop the Russians now, and on May 2, the Berlin Commander, Weidling, gave in, together with 70,000 men. More than 100,000 Germans had been killed.

Meanwhile great events were taking place in every Allied sector. In Italy the long campaign was finished when nearly one million Germans agreed to lay down their arms to Field-Marshal

IN BERLIN. *Russian tanks lumber through piles of rubble as the Germans in the capital continue to hold out against Marshal Zhukov's final onslaught on the city.*

Alexander on May 2. In Germany itself the British armies had taken the strongly-defended town of Bremen and also received the surrender of Hamburg. On May 4, Field-Marshal Montgomery received a delegation of German officers who agreed to unconditional surrender of the German forces in north-west Germany, Holland and Denmark. In Prague, capital of Czecho-Slovakia, the patriots had risen and seized most of the city, upon which General Patton's American troops were driving at full speed, while Russian forces were approaching from the east.

It was now only a matter of hours, and early on the morning of May 7, General Bedell Smith, Chief of Staff to General Eisenhower, entered a small school-room at Rheims to receive Germany's unconditional surrender. In Berlin, on the following day, Field-Marshal Keitel bowed his stiff Prussian neck to sign the same terms in the presence of the Russians. The war in the west was won.

By this time the Nazi leaders were either dead or fugitives. Admiral Doenitz had announced Hitler's death in Berlin during a broadcast on the night of May 1 ; Doenitz had proclaimed himself Chief of the German State and Fuehrer of the nation. The body of Goebbels was found by the Russians in a Berlin air-raid shelter, dead from poison. Himmler, who had attempted, as " the only sane man left in Germany," to make a deal with the Allies, fled in disguise. When captured, he swallowed deadly poison and was interred in an unmarked grave upon a lonely heath. Goering, still fat but no longer jovial, fell into the hands of the Americans. The curtain fell on the last vestiges of Nazi power when Doenitz and his " government " were arrested at Flensburg by the Allies.

One by one the Nazi strongpoints were overwhelmed, despite the exhortations of Goebbels and Hitler, who were in the Chancellery, which the Russians finally captured.

HAMBURG GIVES IN. *This photograph shows the destruction of the streets in Hamburg, the great German port, overrun by British troops in the final stages of their advance.*

Most of the damage had been caused by the tremendous air battering which the city, and particularly its docks, had received by repeated Allied bombing attacks all through the war.

HISTORIC CLIMAX. *German delegates at Montgomery's headquarters on May 4 hear the unconditional terms for their armies in north-west Germany, Holland and Denmark.*

Holding the paper in his hands is General-Admiral von Friedeburg, Commander-in-Chief of the German Navy, with two lesser officers. Friedeburg later committed suicide.

GERMAN ARMIES SURRENDER UNCONDITIONALLY. (*Top left*), *Lieutenant-General W. Bedell Smith signs the armistice agreement at Rheims on May 7, 1945, on behalf of General Eisenhower.* (*Bottom left*), *Colonel-General Jodl signs at Rheims on behalf of the German General Staff.* (*Above*), *Lieutenant-General Charles Foulkes (left) reads surrender orders covering the German armies in Holland to General Blaskowitz (right centre).* (*Below*), *At Caserta, on April 29, a German agent in civilian clothes reads through terms for the Germans in Italy presented by Lieut.-Gen. W. D. Morgan.*

JOURNEY'S END. *The scene is a building in a Berlin suburb, in the early hours of the morning on May 8, 1945. With his cap and field-marshal's baton thrown on the table before him, Field-Marshal Keitel (Chief of the German Army High Command) scrawls his signature to the Russian copy of the surrender document. Among those in the room, which was draped with Allied flags, were Marshal Zhukov, who signed for the Russians, Air Chief Marshal Tedder, representing the Allied Expeditionary Force, with Lieutenant-General Spaatz and General de Lattre de Tassigny as witnesses.*

Copyright S.745V.
Made and Printed in Great Britain by C. Tinling & Co., Ltd., Liverpool, London, and Prescot.